T0197743

GARY L. HAUCK

THE STORY OF HERITAGE VILLAGE

CELEBRATING 25 YEARS

iUniverse, Inc.
Bloomington

The Story of Heritage Village
Celebrating 25 Years

iUniverse books may be ordered through booksellers or by contacting:

iUniverse
1663 Liberty Drive
Bloomington, IN 47403
www.iuniverse.com
1-800-Authors (1-800-288-4677)

ISBN: 978-1-4620-2550-3 (sc)
ISBN: 978-1-4620-2551-0 (e)

Printed in the United States of America

iUniverse rev. date: 7/12/2011

Dedicated to:

The loving memory of all the
departed friends of Heritage Village –
whose labor of love and selfless commitment
have helped to make Heritage Village
what it is today.

Contents

Preface		ix
Acknowledgments		xiii
Introduction – Montcalm Community College		xv
1.	EARLY BEGINNINGS, SHOEN LOG HOUSE, GAFFIELD SCHOOL, AND ASSOCIATION	1
2.	SIDNEY TOWN HALL	15
3.	SIDNEY GENERAL STORE AND THORLAND ICE HOUSE	27
4.	TOOL SHED AND STUMPING MACHINE	33
5.	EDMORE JAIL	37
6.	TREBIAN ORCHARD, GARDENS, ENTRANCE, CEMETERY, AND FARM MACHINE SHED (GIFT SHOP)	43
7.	CABOOSE, WATER TOWER, AND MAINTENANCE OF WAY HANDCAR HOUSE	49
8.	RUSH DAIRY	55
9.	MCBRIDE'S DEPOT	59
10.	PAVILION AND BANDSTAND	63
11.	STEAM ENGINE #7456	67
12.	DOCTOR'S HOUSE	71
13.	BELLE'S HAT SHOPPE AND DELL'S BARBERSHOP	75
14.	BLACKSMITH SHOP	79
15.	PRINT SHOP	83
16.	VILLAGE CHURCH	85
17.	EHLE BARN	91
18.	HERITAGE FESTIVAL AND SANTA'S SUPER SUNDAY	95
19.	THE PRESENT AND FUTURE OF HERITAGE VILLAGE	103
20.	MEET SOME OF THE COMMITTEE MEMBERS & VOLUNTEERS	107
21.	CONTRIBUTORS, MEMBERS, AND VOLUNTEERS	127
	Epilogue – Montcalm Community College Today	135
	Works Cited	139
	About the Author	143

Preface

It was during the fall of 2005 when I first laid eyes on the small cluster of quaint historical buildings just east of Sidney, Michigan, on County Road 510. I was the Director of Academic Affairs for the Grand Rapids Campus of the University of Phoenix, and was scheduled to meet with Dr. Don Burns, the President of Montcalm Community College to work out details for an "articulation agreement" between our two schools. As I parked my car across the street from the steam train, depot, country church, and other preserved structures, I entered the college's Administration/Library Building with many new questions now on my mind.

After exchanging pleasantries, I asked Dr. Burns, "What is that village across the street?"

"That's actually on our campus property," he replied. "We call it 'Heritage Village.' It has quite a story. Maybe sometime you can visit during our annual festival, and you can explore it more carefully!"

We continued our meeting about curricular matters, but given my passion for history I found myself wanting inwardly to focus the conversation on this new discovery of mine. It wasn't until the summer of 2008 that I had my opportunity to explore as the college president suggested.

I had just returned to Michigan after leading a study abroad group to Great Britain, said farewell to my friends at the University of Phoenix, and joined the administrative team at Montcalm Community College as the dean of arts and sciences. While still getting my office unpacked and settled in, Dr. Burns came over and exclaimed, "You know, Heritage Festival begins in just a few days. You need to go over and check it out!"

So, on Thursday morning, August 7, 2008, I had the wonderful opportunity to enter the log cabin, observe children studying in the old school house, meander through the doctor's house, examine the goods in the amazing country store, and reflect in the serene country church. Each building had a gracious and informative docent donned in period dress. With the activities in full swing and people milling about the village, I felt transported into the past. I returned on Friday, and made the hour's drive again on Saturday to take pictures of the Civil War re-enactors, talk with the tanner, ask questions of the printer, enjoy the musicians on the bandstand, grab a hot dog at the pavilion, savor ice cream in the dairy, and get a history lesson in the old town hall. I was hooked.

At the country store I met Jean Brundage, a trustee of the college and Chairperson of the Heritage Village Committee and Association who invited me to attend one of the monthly meetings. And, as soon as I got my bearings on my new position, I began attending and joined the association myself. I was absolutely amazed at the dedication and hard work of the volunteers and Committee members. Though almost all of them were retired and somewhat advanced in years, they had a sparkle and youthfulness about them that emitted a sense of vision, purpose, and strong commitment!

Soon, I found myself acting in costume as a substitute schoolmaster at the schoolhouse, docent of the Village Church, and promoter of the village at large. On March 12, 2010, I had the pleasure of performing the wedding ceremony of my oldest son and his bride in the Village Church. Both her family and mine enjoyed the perfect setting of the village despite the cloudy and drizzly March skies. Later, for Festival 2010, the Committee asked me to serve as the coordinator and host of the Bob Milne Ragtime Concert and Hymn Sing. Committee members Dr. Eugene Rydahl and Ron Springsteen also approached me about the possibility of introducing a local history and heritage course into the curriculum of Montcalm Community College. Happily, I was able to draft the course and present it to the Social Science Department and college curriculum committee for approval. HIST 256 "Local History and Heritage" will be offered on location at the Village for the first time during the eight-week summer session of 2011.

In October of 2010, the Committee began discussing the possibility of putting together some sort of written history of the Village for the upcoming 25th anniversary year. Tom Learmont asked if there were any college students who might like to tackle the project. We discussed the size and extent of the project, and determined that it might be difficult to find a student willing to take on that task. It was during one of those conversations that I chose to volunteer my own services for the project. At an upcoming meeting of the

Committee, the members affirmed the decision, and I began to accumulate all the information I could.

I decided to begin the process by interviewing Chairperson Jean Brundage, MCC President Emeritus Don Burns, Vice President for Administrative Services Jim Lantz, and Committee Member Tom Learmont. Next, I sent "written interview questions" to every past and present member of the Committee. I read through hundreds of pages of Committee minutes provided by Terry Smith (Director of Institutional Advancement and former Village Committee Secretary), Town Hall scrapbooks, and Sidney Township records. Finally, I made numerous phone calls and had several follow-up conversations. Although I took notes and typed reflections all along the process, I took the Spring Break of 2011 to write the rough draft, and shared it with Mr. Lantz, Ms. Brundage, Ms. Kim Bell of the college's English department, Ms. Jane LaLonde (MCC Administrative Assistant for Academic Affairs), Shelly Strautz-Springborn (Public Information Coordinator), my wife, Lois, and several others, for critique, corrections, and review.

Serving as both a temporary local historian and historiographer has been a serious and somewhat daunting responsibility. I apologize in advance for any volunteer work that may have gone unreported, names that I may have failed to recognize, or events that may have been slighted. My attempt has been a sincere one. To the best of my ability, I have sought to tell the story of Heritage Village as accurately and objectively as possible with what resources I was able to find and use.

I discovered in the process that the story of Heritage Village is not simply a story of buildings, amazing as they are. This is a story about people – those who lived in and among these structures in days gone by, and those who have labored to reconstruct and preserve them, and bring them to life. It is the fabric of these individual narratives that has been woven together to make *The Story of Heritage Village*. On this very day, we had the privilege of conducting the initial tour of this special season for students, instructors, staff members, and members of the community at large. We enjoyed sharing many of these narratives to this august group, and now we enjoy sharing them with you. During this 25th anniversary year, we celebrate and salute everyone who has had a hand in making Heritage Village what it is today!

Gary L. Hauck
May 3, 2011

Acknowledgments

I owe a debt of gratitude to the many people who had a part in this research process. There are some who made special contributions. I would like to thank Dr. Don Burns, Mr. Jim Lantz, Ms. Jean Brundage, and Mr. Tom Learmont for graciously granting me extensive personal interviews. I also wish to thank the Heritage Village Committee members and friends of both the past and the present who took the time to respond to my written interview questions, and contributed much pertinent information.

These individuals include: Kathleen Beard, Larry Beard, Ruth Bedore, Jean Brundage, Robert Buskirk, Geraldine Christensen, Lillian Christophersen, Jesse Fox, Marilyn Fox, Maxine Harris, Vivien Hey, Tom Learmont, Mildred Mahan, Bob Marston, Jim Paris, Flora Phelps, Max Phelps, Sharon Ritter, Alvin Rush, Margaret Rush, Dr. Eugene Rydahl, Dr. William Seiter, Barney Shoen, Ilene Thomsen, Marge Waldren, Evelyn Warner, Dale White, Judy White, Mrs. Valgene Mack, and Miriam Zimmerman.

I am grateful to the entire Heritage Village Association Committee for entrusting me with this project, and to the administrative support staff at Montcalm Community College for good assistance. Special appreciation is extended to Jane LaLonde for her help with the questionnaire mailings, and April Keeler for her assistance with the preparation of the list of the contributors, members, and volunteers.

On a more personal note, I wish to thank my wife, Lois, for proofreading each of the drafts, and for her willingness to have a preoccupied husband for these past several months. I also thank my son, Jared, for his many hours of assistance with the photos and creation of the black and white collages from the many pictures I have taken over the past three years. Special thanks also go to Mr. Dale White, Ms. Maxine Harris, and Mr. Jim Paris, for providing original photographs from years gone by, and to Jody Hedrick and Shelly

Strautz-Springborn for photos of student tour groups and the contemporary Village map.

Finally, I thank Kim Bell and Shelly Strautz-Springborn for their grammatical refinements and suggestions, Dr. Joel Brouwer for his assistance with MLA citation style, Tom Learmont for additional personnel information, Terry Smith for access to the original Committee minutes, and Heritage Village Chairperson Jean Brundage for her overall support and assistance.

Introduction –
Montcalm Community College

During the early 1960s, a group of Montcalm County citizens conceived of the idea of creating a community college in the area. A planning committee organized, and a contest was begun to determine the name of the new institution. David Pritchard and Dorthea Krampe tied in the contest with the name, Montcalm Community College. On March 2, 1965, the school was officially established, a board of trustees was elected, and classes began in several high school buildings in the county. Because of its central location in Montcalm County, the site of the farm of Alma and Ernie Anderson was chosen for the school's campus, just east of Sidney on Sidney Road. On Monday, September 26, 1966, Governor George Romney officiated at the ground-breaking ceremony near the Anderson farmhouse. Also presiding at the festivities were Charles Simon of Stanton, and Stanley Ash, Chairman of the newly established College. Dr. Donald Fink was invited to become the school's first president. Dr. Fink was followed by Dr. Herbert Stoutenburg, Dr. Clifford Bedore, and then by Dr. Donald Burns (Olson, *North Sidney* 41).

By 1986, the 240-acre campus had a cluster of buildings and well over a thousand students in both credit and non-credit courses. Varieties of programs were offered for both occupational and transfer students, leading to both certificates and degrees. MCC became accredited by the Higher Learning Commission of the North Central Association, and established its mission as "a learning community in which educated and trained people contribute to the economic, cultural and social well-being" (*MCC Catalog* 5).

It was during this twentieth year of the campus, 1986, that a new concept emerged – the formation of an historic village on the College property. The birth of this idea cannot be credited to any one individual, but by a confluence of interests that remarkably took hold at the same time. Yet, everyone who had a part in those early roots had one desire in common – to preserve the heritage of the past as a learning tool for the future. For this reason, it is most appropriate that the name given to this creative venue would come to be, "Heritage Village." This is *The Story of Heritage Village – Celebrating 25 Years!*

The Gaffield School and Shoen Log House at
Heritage Village in Sidney, Michigan.

1.

EARLY BEGINNINGS, SHOEN LOG HOUSE, GAFFIELD SCHOOL, AND ASSOCIATION

The story of Heritage Village in Sidney, Michigan, is a fascinating one with a humble beginning, an evolving vision, and the amazing dedication of volunteer thinkers, movers, shakers, and workers. It was birthed on the campus of Montcalm Community College in 1986, and has maintained a symbiotic union ever since. Although it is an independent association, Heritage Village rests on the campus of MCC, and enjoys an active partnership with administrators, faculty members, staff and students, as well as the community at large.

In the most fascinating confluence of factors, the idea of an historic village on the campus of MCC emerged twenty-five years ago as: 1.) Four women: Rosemary Long, Maxine Harris, Mildred Mahan, and Hazel Smith, traveled to Ludington to visit The Historic White Pine Village. When they returned, they thought they could copy the idea and this would be a wonderful addition to MCC's campus. 2.) The Shoen family of Crystal was hoping to preserve the heritage of its family log house, and explored the possibility of MCC's interest in acquiring it. 3.) Dr. William Seiter, the Superintendent of the Montcalm Area Intermediate School District, belonged to an organization seeking a way to preserve a one-room school house as an historical/educational tool for future generations. 4.) The State of Michigan was looking for creative ways to celebrate its upcoming sesquicentennial and local committee members sought a unique way to do that in Montcalm County.

The Shoen Log House

In the summer of 1986, the Shoen family of nearby Crystal, Michigan, approached MCC's president, Dr. Donald C. Burns, with an offer (first discussed as early as 1979) to donate its family log cabin constructed in 1860 to become an historic fixture on the college property. The Shoen siblings explained that it belonged to their parents, and was the home that carried their childhood memories. Burns recalls:

> The family contacted me and wanted to give the log building. My understanding was that it was a barn. Quite frankly, I didn't 'get it.' But it's a wonderful example of the community's participation of community relationship with the college. Hazel Smith was very excited about the idea of capturing history, and she and others had this amazing imagination. She was just a community member – that is to say, not a member of the college. (That's the beauty of this. It was from the grassroots of the community. We align with and enhance the community and community activities. It develops as it should when you are open to ideas that are beyond what you think from the inside out and this is a great example of that. They saw something that could be a reality — a cultural venue — by capturing pieces of history and bringing them and people together to celebrate our heritage.) So the first discussions basically were, 'Here's a building, what do you think?' I was thinking, 'How are we going to take care of this? It's going to just sit out there. What are you going to do with it?' (Burns)

Despite some of his doubts, Dr. Burns went to see the structure as a result of an "emergency call." "Please come over here," one of the Schoen family members said strongly over the phone. Burns was told they had to get rid of it and were going to burn it down. The family was pleading, "Please, can't you take it? We really don't want to see it go." So, Burns looked it over. After he saw it, Burns realized it had been a house that was transformed into a barn. He also quickly realized that it couldn't be moved, but rather would have to be taken apart piece by piece and put back together.

After giving this offer some thought, Dr. Burns asked Vice President James Lantz, and Director of Facilities Frank Reeder to visit and examine the log building, situated just west of the town of Crystal. Mr. Lantz recalls:

When Frank and I went to look at the Shoen log house, we were surprised to see a fairly good-sized structure with more than one room. It was somewhat of a bi-level structure, with one room as one story, and one section having a room and a half. It was covered by siding over the years, and the area around it was quite overgrown with weeds and brush. We looked around and said, "This is really a neat structure." We did see some rot in some of the logs, but thought, "Okay, if the college wants it, let's do it." (Lantz)

Frank was later joined by Jesse Fox and Bill Raymor who spoke with Ken Lehman, the owner of Big L Lumber in Greenville and a strong supporter and generous donor of the college. (Mr. Lehman also contributed to the development of the nature trails, which now bear his name.) Ken offered to donate the necessary equipment and personnel to move the log cabin to the west lot of MCC in Sidney. With all this information in hand, Dr. Burns asked Jesse Fox to make the official arrangements to accept the Log House, and proceed with the project.

In preparation for the process of dismantling and moving the structure, Lantz developed a code to mark all of the logs so they could be reassembled properly. Frank and his custodial staff acquired some little metal tags (bearing a series of letters and numbers) to identify each log, and nailed a tag to each piece. He also crafted a drawing of the structure for the purpose of careful reconstruction. Several MCC employees volunteered to help move the cabin, but those from Big L did most of the work. Lantz again recalls,

> Big L got a truck to transport it, and a fork lift to move the logs one by one as the structure was first disassembled, loaded on the truck, brought here, and then put back together. Most of the MCC folks watched. (Lantz)

At the time, the college had a couple of custodians who had some interest and skill in rebuilding projects -- Gaylerd Cooper, who once served in the Navy's Construction Brigade, and Gary Kieffer, the uncle of today's MCC Information Systems Director, Rod Middleton. They were the ones who actually reconstructed the house during the spring of 1987. As they began, they discovered that many of the logs were rotted and not usable. "We had to acquire some logs from a log barn in Sheridan to supplement, but could not get enough to rebuild it exactly the way it was," Lantz explains. President Burns talked to the Shoen family about this dilemma, who felt very disappointed. Their hope was to reconstruct it exactly as it stood in Crystal. But according to Lantz, "There wasn't anything else we could do. So we began to construct it as a one room log cabin. The logs are a combination of the good logs from the original cabin and some of the good logs from the barn." The second level was therefore eliminated. Local citizen Bill Lacy helped to find replacement logs, and it was Jean Brundage who told them of the barn on Holland Lake Road, north of Sheridan, owned by the Christopherson family, who happily donated the barn for logs. Ed Minnion, a member of the MCC Maintenance Staff at the time agreed to build a rock foundation, and other volunteers offered to build a new replacement roof.

The reconstruction team also used *chinking* (mortar that lasts) to insert between the logs. Mr. Lantz did some searching (primarily in magazines, since the internet had not yet become widely accessible), and discovered a company in Tennessee called Perma-Chink that developed a product with elastic ability to expand and shrink with the heat and cold. Before applying the Perma-Chinck, the workers drove steel rods down through the logs to keep them in place. The college paid for the chinking, and because the maintenance crew was less busy in the summer, the college allowed Cooper and Kieffer to reconstruct the log house during normal working hours.

Finally, it was completed. To commemorate this event, the college held an "open house" and invited the Shoen family members as the honored guests. Once they heard Dr. Burns' description of the process and arrived on campus to see the reconstructed Shoen Log House for themselves, they were pleased. Mildred Mahan was present when the Shoen family made the official presentation to MCC, and remembers how family members gave some interesting facts and stories about how the log house was used (Mahan). A plaque was presented to them as well, which is now located in the old Log House. It reads, "Montcalm Community College would like to extend a special thank you to Clifford Shoen and his wife Leta, and his sisters, Alta and Velma, for the donation of this historical structure in memory of Barney and Elizabeth Shoen." It also states, "The house stands in Heritage Village as a monument to Montcalm County's early days."

Volunteers set out to fill the cabin with items reminiscent of some of those stories. To furnish it, a rope bed and dresser were donated by Phil Frisbie, who later became the village historian. According to Brundage, Phil did a lot of research and work (along with his art students at Vestaburg), making quilts, paper-mâché items, crochet doilies, and woven rugs, and even taught classes on arts and crafts in the log cabin. Frisbie also made "hair flowers," and explained how pictures made of the hair of grandparents would be passed down through the generations (Brundage interview).

In a letter dated February 19, 2011, Barney A. Shoen writes, "Although I am too old to remember many of the details, I do remember being reared in that Log House. It holds many special memories." Shoen is happy that it is now a part of Heritage Village, and says that the old cabin "speaks for itself." Some of those memories were captured in a newspaper article titled, "Area Couples Celebrate 75 Years of Marital Bliss," written by Linda Christensen of *The Daily News* [Greenville] and published on Thursday, January 16, 1997:

> **CRYSTAL** – He was 18 years of age; she 16; he wore a coffee colored suit; she a handmade dress – together they road from Crystal to Stanton in a Model T-Ford on January 28, 1922, a beautiful, sunny day – their wedding day.
>
> The couple, Clifford and Leta Shoen, lifelong residents of Crystal, will soon be celebrating that special day during their 75th wedding anniversary party with family and friends on January 26th.
>
> "I remember the day so well," Leta said, "It was real cold, but beautiful and sunny." The ceremony, which was short, she said, included a couple of women who worked in the Pastor's office as witnesses. After the ceremony, the couple returned home to a small house next door to the Shoen family farm.
>
> The Shoens eventually expanded their family by having four children, two boys and two girls and later moved into the log cabin which had been built back in 1860. The cabin, which originally sported a second story, is now on display at the Heritage Village in Sidney. (Christensen)

Ilene Thomsen was one of the first volunteers to work in the Shoen Log House, and donated many of the items that are now on display there. She says that when children used to visit the Log House, they seemed to always ask the same three questions: Where are the bathrooms? Where is the bedroom? What is the water pail for? Her answers were, "Outside restrooms; the loft was not put in when the cabin was moved; and most everyone drank water from the water pail with a dipper" (Thomsen). Ilene was also joined by Mildred Mahan and Maxine Harris. Maxine writes, "When the children came through, I was one of those who had the fun of explaining the contents and their uses to them. They were so interested and asked so many good questions. They seemed most fascinated by the spinning wheel, feather bed, baby crib, dad's red flannels, old Sears catalogs, button shoes, soap stone (foot heater), kitchen sink, pail-dipper, and rotary towel" (Harris).

Ironically, The Shoen Log House is now Dr. Burn's favorite. "My great grandparents had a place like this that I used to see as a youngster. They built it in the 1870s and it was much like this, a wooden building. And now I see the wisdom in acquiring this structure" (Burns).

Kathy Beard serves as today's volunteer in charge of the Shoen Log House. She shares:

> I volunteered to be responsible for the Log House when Edna Hansen, who was responsible for it, was unable to continue due to health concerns. That was in early 2007. Since it was built in 1860, we have many items that were used in the 1860s in the Log House that make it interesting to people of all ages to see; sometimes they try to figure out what they were used for. I always tell the children about the chamber pot and get their reaction. I also ask them if they know what the rug beater is, and get all kinds of answers! The most popular answers are fly swatter and something used to spank misbehaving children. I enjoy listening to the older women tell about using some of the things in the cabin when they were younger. (K. Beard)

The Gaffield School

In between the early discussions of the log house and its reconstruction at MCC, the first building moved to the campus property was actually the one-room school house. Dr. Burns remembers a phone call he received in 1986 from Dr. William Seiter, Superintendent of the Montcalm Area Intermediate School District. Dr. Seiter asked Burns if he had any interest in obtaining the school, known as The Gaffield School (located just south of Amble), and offered to help provide some of the money to move it. Constructed in 1904, the school was an excellent example of how one teacher taught all the children from beginners to the eighth grade. It was still furnished with the desks that varied in size from the very tiny to those accommodating taller adolescents.

Dr. Seiter writes, "I was a member of MARSP, a formal organization of 'retired' teachers interested in obtaining a one-room school to be maintained as an example of early rural education in Michigan" (Seiter). He continues, "I vividly recall memories of the efforts and energies involved in obtaining and getting the unit moved to Heritage Village."

For Dr. Burns, this acquisition made instant sense, since it was educationally related. A decision was quickly made, and the building was donated by its owners at the time, David and Phyllis Larsen. It was moved to its present site in 1986, just before the arrival of the Log House project.

Bob Marston, MCC Trustee and then counselor for the Montcalm Area Intermediate School District, assisted in moving the structure and preparing the site at Heritage Village. He writes, "I worked for MAISD at the time, and there was a real commitment to helping our area celebrate Michigan's 150th anniversary of becoming a state. Since I was selected as chair for the Sesquicentennial Committee and was also on the board at MCC, I was especially interested in this project. It was the first building to be moved to the campus, and being a school, it made good sense" (Marston).

Jean Brundage, MCC Trustee and Chair of the Heritage Village Association, remembers how the building was literally moved on a flat-bed truck. She also recalls,

> After moving it here, we added a large, black heating stove that used either wood or coal, and a piano that was a gift of the Baptist church in Crystal. Al Gooding donated the clock on the wall and put pictures on the back wall of actual prior classes at the school. Other items were furnished by retired school teachers. During our first celebration, Eva Main served as our 'teacher,' with a curriculum written by Geraldine Christensen, Eleanor Lentz, and Jean Zimmerman. Phil Frisbie taught the second year, and then Eleanor Lentz became our regular teacher. She was the eldest of twelve children, and actually went to a one-room school house! Edna Hansen, an instructor in MCC's speech department at the time, was also among the first teachers, and helped with the school. Sharon Ritter continues that custom today, donned in her period costume, and teaches school-age children during the annual Heritage Festival. (Brundage interview)

Sharon Ritter exclaims, "It has been such a pleasure to take over as teacher when Eleanor Lentz felt she had to step down. I guess the building chose me! I also attended a one-room school as a child, and always wanted to teach. After attending MCC toward my degree, I taught in a building somewhat like this for three years back in the 50s. One person now owns that old school!" (Ritter). She continues, "I always enjoy speaking with adults who come through the school house during Festival as well. Many share their own memories of attending one-room schools." Sharon likes to call their attention to the many photos on the back wall of one-room schools in the area, the map showing where over a hundred old schools were located, and the many books that were actually used over the years.

Miriam Zimmerman also assists at Gaffield School during school tours, sharing the "teacher" duties with Ms. Ritter. Miriam shares, "Since I had been a classroom teacher, Jean Brundage naturally felt it would be a good fit for me as well. It's enjoyable to try to get the children to imagine the limitations of a one-room school, and yet the community feel of it by those families attending" (Zimmerman letter).

A flier for the 1987 Heritage Village Celebration at the school read:

Welcome to our one-room rural school in Heritage Village, Sidney, Michigan. As you enter please step back in time to the 1920s and early 1930s. Let's pretend that Calvin Coolidge is our president. Alexander Groesbeck is our governor. Our flag has 48 stars and we say our pledge differently...

We hope your visit will be stimulating and interesting. The school house is not yet completely restored. Our dream is that Heritage Village will grow and be a means of enrichment for our children and a source of joy and refreshment to those for whom it is a "Memory Lane." (Heritage Village, *School Days*)

By 1995, the building had been completely restored, but the paint on the school was badly peeling and some of the siding needed to be replaced. So, in his early years at the Village, Tom Learmont took on the project of scraping the building, repairing the siding and then painting the building. Over the next 10 years, Tom made other repairs and organized a group to repaint the school again. In 2008, the Association hired a painter to redo the school for the third time. Learmont also took the lead in hiring a contractor to install the current shingled roof.

The structure of the school house at Heritage Village is somewhat reminiscent of the first school house constructed in Sidney during the year of 1858, built by volunteers and supervised by the founder of the township, Joshua Noah (Olson, *North Sidney* 32). Lillian Christophersen shares:

> My mother, Alma Corfixsen, was a teacher at the Sidney School (in the 30s, I think). She was instrumental in getting the merry-go-round as the students had nothing to play on. (The swings were put there when I attended in the 40s and early 50s.) When the Township Board was going to take it out of the park, I asked if I could have it. But when they said it was going to Heritage Village, I was happy. It had a warped board on it when I was a kid. We called it "the slippery board" because we could slide off it.
>
> I have given boxes of old school books and supplies that belonged to my mother. I also gave my mother's class picture from County Normal and her old valentines from the 1930s. (Christopersen)

One of the favorite items in the school house is an actual photograph of the Gaffield School taken of the students in the academic year of 1915-1916, with teacher Doris Mulholland. It is located on the north wall inside the classroom.

The Heritage Village Association

When the village began, the college was also involved in a grant-funded program called *Montcalm Tomorrow*, intended to be a visioning group to plan the future direction of Montcalm County in all its aspects. Mr. Les Morford served as the executive director while serving on the MCC faculty. Inspired by a vision of what the Shoen Log Cabin and Gaffield School projects could become, several retired individuals in the area began to dream of an entire historic village. Colleagues lovingly and humorously referred to this group as *Montcalm Yesterday!* Mrs. Hazel Smith, a public school teacher from the community, became the first chair of the newly formed association of volunteers, and the official name of "Heritage Village" was adopted. In a letter written in July of 1988, Hazel wrote, "We believe Heritage Village is an important part of our community, serving as a permanent monument to our history" (Smith, Official minutes). A mission statement and a constitution were also drafted by these committee members. Their goal was to get other buildings for the village and make it a life-size museum of Montcalm

County's heritage. "This organization shall be dedicated to the preservation of the history of the Montcalm County area. In achieving this purpose, the organization will work toward the following specific goals:

A.   To establish a village where children and adults may learn and enjoy the life of early times.

B.   To preserve the past by restoring original buildings or replicating original ones.

C.   To preserve the stories, history and data through written, oral and pictoral histories.

D.   To conduct an annual "Heritage Village Celebration."

E.   To provide a setting where school children may experience an early classroom.

F.   To encourage community groups to use and support Heritage Village.

G.   To promote the village as a historically significant attraction in the county.

H.   To promote activities that will create and support continued interest in the preservation of the history of the area." (Heritage Village, *Constitution* II:1)

Hazel's son, Peter Smith, developed a concept drawing of what the village could eventually become, including a church, store, and all the key structures that would have comprised a typical village during the time span of 1860-1910. Although this plan was adopted, future acquisitions (including the locomotive, for example) would change the range from 1860 to 1926.

Jean Brundage shares, "Tom Learmont developed a master plan for us, and later contracted a gentleman who did the landscaping at Amway to draft a more detailed drawing, which he did without charge. It was a great big thing that hung in Jesse Fox's garage until we moved it into the depot" (Brundage interview). But it was Jesse Fox that designed the original sketch of the future village on October 3, 1986, so that the MCC board would have an idea of the vision before approving it. He writes, "The MCC Board wanted some idea of what the finished product would look like before they would approve the idea. This sketch included ideas from several committee members" (J. Fox letter).

(A copy of the third and final draft of this sketch is seen at the beginning of chapter 20 [top of photo].)

As plans developed and the vision became enlarged, a Native American village was also considered, but that idea was put on hold indefinitely. Since these early beginnings, several other buildings have been added or constructed as re-creations. And while all desired to keep the village as true to life as possible, electricity and running water were later added to accommodate today's needs.

Beatrice Doser was serving as Chair of the Board at Montcalm Community College at the time and asked Trustee Jean Brundage to join this committee to represent the college. Jean started as the first official secretary, then became vice chair, then chair following Hazel Smith, who faithfully led the committee for its first four years of existence. During this time, the committee had grown to some 20-30 individuals from the community, with no other personnel from the college except Terry Smith, who also served as secretary. After Brundage became the chair, she decided to designate people to each building, providing a strong sense of ownership and ongoing creativity. Elenor Lentz was assigned to the school and Lillian Hansen to the log cabin, followed by Maxine Harris, Edna Hansen, and Kathy Beard. Brundage has steadily chaired the Heritage Village Committee until the present day.

The zealous body of volunteers raised money to acquire and move buildings from across the county to the Heritage Village site, with the understanding that once they were moved, they would become part of the college property. Association volunteers held spaghetti dinners and quilt raffles to raise money for each building, which cost between $10,000 – $20,000 to move! A large part of this sum was paid to the utility companies to take down or hold up power wires as flat bed trucks transported the school, Sidney Township Hall, and others.

Heritage Village Association remains an independent group operating with the college's blessing to promote, celebrate, and expand. Burns explains:

> As it emerged over the years, it continued to be a wonderful example of the relationship between the community and the college and community ownership. I'm aware of museums owned by community colleges that have their own staff run it and pay for it. Here, the individual community members and the Heritage Village Committee took ownership, and what you see here today – every one of these

pieces, came with the toil and sweat of community members. The log cabin is not the only one that was taken apart. The Ehle barn was also taken apart and rebuilt here. The volunteers put it back together so quickly, that people didn't realize it was here! It fit so well! The wood was so nicely aged, and it fit so well, it was here for awhile before people realized it. Because members of the committee have this sense of ownership, they keep these building in repair. They don't wait for them to deteriorate. They repair them, they paint them, they update them, and they have a schedule for all of this. (Burns).

Burns is grateful for the nature of the relationship with the college. He continues to view the Heritage Village Committee as a "gold mine." "All these people with knowledge, energy, and history coupled with such a positive attitude keep it continually getting better. And it's a work in progress, all the time."

The Gaffield School in its original setting near Amble. The 1915-1916 Students of Gaffield School. Sharon Ritter teaches the school children during Festival. The School exterior at Heritage Village. Elle Kemph in the Shoen Log House. Interior of the Log House. Edna Hansen instructs a school touring group during Heritage Village's Spring Educational Tours.

Members of the Benson and Gommesen families walk past the Town Hall in period costume. Town Hall exterior and interior. Alvin and Margaret Rush muse with Ron Springsteen following a Town Hall re-enactment. Gene Rydahl takes a moment to rest after directing the Town Hall drama during Festival.

2.

SIDNEY TOWN HALL

Earl Christiansen was a faculty member at the college who brought computers to MCC. It is somewhat ironic that an Information Technology instructor would be instrumental in acquiring both the town hall and the store. According to Burns, Earl was a "worldly wise, well-traveled, globally connected entrepreneur and instructor, who created the college's IT curriculum that began as non-credit, and developed into a full-credit department. His wife was from the area as well, and also taught at MCC. They played a key role in our acquiring of the Sidney Town Hall for Heritage Village, and also donated the store" (Burns).

In fact, both Sidney Town Hall (built in the late 1800's) and the Sidney General Store were acquired at the same time. In 1989, the structure was owned by Sidney State Bank and used for meetings, since it was situated just north of the bank on Derby Road. The bank generously donated the building at no cost to the Village, and covered the cost to move it to the Heritage Village site. According to Mr. Jim Paris, the current president of Sidney State Bank, "The bank was planning at that time to use the site for other purposes and the timing was right." He states, "I and the two presidents that preceded me, Rex Rice and Steve Shoen, are all proud of our bank's involvement with Heritage Village, as is our entire board of directors" (Paris). (Interestingly, Mr. Paris has also worked in the Village gardens as a master gardener, and his daughter acted as one of the students in the school house when she was in junior high.)

In addition to the costs of transporting the building to its new location as alluded to earlier, money was also needed for the power company that would temporarily take down or prop up the power lines as was necessary when moving the school. To raise the additional funds needed, members were invited to join the Heritage Village Association for a donation of $10.00 per year or $100.00 for life. The committee rigorously planned numerous spaghetti dinners and bake sales, and raised the needed money in a remarkable period of time. A mover from Alma was contracted to literally transport the structure on a flatbed truck, and the day finally arrived. Very dramatically, the truck made its way south on Derby Road and turned the corner onto Sidney Road, making the two-plus mile trek to its current location.

The building still has a slight list because of a prior tornado that stormed through the area. According to *The Story of North Sidney Area 1884-1984,* "…on Tuesday, the 12th of June, 1902, there was a terrible storm over the entire community. Trees were uprooted, fences moved, buildings twisted and St. John's church which had stood high upon the hill was destroyed by the tornado" (Olson, *North Sidney* 4). This may very likely have been the storm that caused the damage to the town hall. As is, the old hall was placed on a block foundation, but had earlier rested on a foundation made of large stones. At the time, Max Simon taught construction classes at Lakeview and volunteered to install stones around the foundation to make it look more authentic. He also painted the building inside and outside.

Other work had to be done. The Town Hall had wood panels on the walls and a dropped ceiling. Volunteers took off the wood panels, and in the process discovered a line where there had been a stage during the earlier years. So, the workers put a stage back into the front of the interior. Originally, there had also been two doors on the rear wall, but now the building could only have one. Creatively, the volunteers removed one of the doors and installed a window in its place. When all of the painting was completed, the transformation was hardly noticeable.

To furnish the Town Hall, many members and friends of the Village made donations, including surrounding townships. A plaque hanging on the south wall inside of the Town Hall lists the items given, and each of the donors:

DONATIONS TO THE TOWN HALL – HERITAGE VILLAGE

BUILDING – SIDNEY STATE BANK

WITH HALL – 1 BENCH AND 1 BALLOT BOX

48 STAR FLAG – CLARENCE OLSON

50 STAR FLAG – AMERICAN LEGION POST 452 – STANTON

BALLOT BOX – VIGGO AND MILDRED HANSEN

CERAMIC EAGLE – PAT DALEY

LUMBER FOR REPAIR – FRANK DREWS

UPRIGHT PIANO AND BENCH – ROBERT SWENSON

2 4x4 TABLES AND 1 4x8 TABLE – MAPLE VALLEY TOWNSHIP

2 VOTING BOOTHS – TRUFANT TOWN HALL

2 VOTING BOOTHS – CORAL TOWN HALL

6 WOODEN BENCHES – OLSONS – FINISHED BY OSBORNS

1 SMALL TABLE FOR DISPLAY – CLARENCE OLSON

TOWNSHIP BOOKS, RECORDS, ETC. – CRYSTAL TOWNSHIP

1 LANTERN – CHARLEY DREWS

MARKING PENCILS – MARIAN RITTER

2 CHAIRS – HARRIET OLSON

1 LAMP – HARRIET OLSON

ASSESSMENT ROLL 1921 SIDNEY TOWNSHIP – FRANK DREWS

ASSESSMENT ROLL – PETER SMITH

COPY OF 1875 COUNTY PLAT MAP, FRAMED WITH TITLE – MARGARETTE HANSEN

OLD TAX RECEIPTS – SECTION 17 & 19 SIDNEY – VIGGO HANSEN

1921 MONTCALM CO. PLAT BOOK – LEAH LARSEN

NOV. 6, 1934 INSTRUCTION BALLOT – PHIL FRISBIE

PENS AND INK AND SEALING WAX – PHIL FRISBIE

CRYSTAL TOWNSHIP SEAL – CRYSTAL TWP. BY JEAN BRUNDAGE

TRUNK FROM HAZELTON FARM – ALBERN OLSON

HISTORY OF MONTCALM COUNTY I & 11 – DASEF – GLEN STOKES FAMILY

FLORENCE HEATING STOVE – HOWELL FAMILY

U.S. WALL MAP – BRYCE CHRISTOFFERSEN & IRENE STOWELL

WALL LAMPS – HAZEL SMITH

BIBLE – RONNIE RASMUSSEN

ATLAS – ERWIN WOERPEL

SONG BOOKS – JOHN CHADWICK

CHAIRS – FRED EHLE

FAMILY BIBLE – DAVID WOODS FAMILY

MONTCALM CO. ATLAS 1897 – PIERSON FAMILY – ELEANOR PORTER

ASSESSMENT ROLL GUIDE FOR STANTON – A. D. NEWMAN

COURT HOUSE STAFF PICTURE – MARVIN NELSON

G. A. R. GAVEL (TOWLE'S) – LEO SCHACHTELE

HISTORICAL SCRAPBOOKS, ATLAS 1898, POSTCARDS – J. R. SWENSON

MONTCALM PLATBOOK AND BOOKS – J. R. SWENSON

SCHOOL DISTRICT RECORDS DISTRICT #5 1905 – VANESSA DREWS

RECORDS DISTRICT #31 1866, 1898, AND 1903 – VANESSA DREWS

SIDNEY TELEPHONE CO. 1906 – VANESSA DREWS

ASSORTED CLIPPINGS – VANESSA DREWS

STORAGE CUPBOARD – TOM LEARMONT

MATERIALS FROM HAZELTON HOUSE – ALBERN OLSON

PANEL DOOR – ALBERN OLSON

Perusing this list, the reader will notice that the gift of one original bench came with the Town Hall building, and that the Olsons built the others to match. Clarence and Harriet Olson were the first members assigned as docents. (Interestingly, Harriet was known to have displayed two different flags on their home in addition to the Stars and Stripes. Since she was a Dane and Clarence was a Swede, she would also hang both the Danish and Swedish flags as well.)

With her experience as a drama teacher, Harriet wrote plays based on characters found in the old recorded minutes and collected artifacts that are still housed today in the glass cases. Some of the books currently on display came from the Crystal Town Hall, and Joyce Ehle (sister-in-law of retired MCC staff member Gene Ehle) obtained some books and a bookcase from the Stanton Courthouse where she worked. Both Joyce and her husband Fred volunteered on many projects for the village. A document kept within the Sidney Town Hall scrapbook summarizes the history of The Town Hall — Sidney Township:

THE TOWN HALL – SIDNEY TOWNSHIP
Location T 10 N Range 7 W

A petition to set aside the above location from Fairplains Township was presented to the Montcalm Board of Supervisors and was approved on January 5, 1857. The name that was chosen was SIDNEY. The first election was ordered at the house of Joshua V. Noah on April 6, 1857. Ira Barlow was elected the first Supervisor and held that office for 7 years. Town meetings were held at different homes or the school house at first. The deed for the ground for the town hall was Jan. 5, 1884. The hall was built about 1888. On Nov. 7, 1888 they met in the township hall for their first election returns. In 1968 the town hall was moved to the next lot north in Sidney. Then on July 27, 1989 it was moved from this place to it's [sic] present site at Montcalm Heritage Village. (Sidney vol. 1:3)

Lillian Christophersen was among those appointed by Hazel Smith to serve on the committee to move the Sidney Town Hall. This was especially meaningful for her because when she was a student at the Sidney School many years ago, one of her favorite activities was to play hopscotch on the big cement slab in front of the town hall. During one of the first years of the town hall's events at the Heritage Festival, Lillian and her husband John were in a play written by Harriet Olson, acting the role of a Danish couple who were married in the Sidney Town Hall. At a subsequent Festival, Lillian sang "Precious Memories" for the opening ceremony. Prior to the construction of the Village Church, opening ceremonies for Festival were conducted in the Town Hall.

The tradition of acting out a town meeting during the annual festival continues to this day, with a different township of Montcalm County being featured every year. For this reason, a temporary sign is added during Festival with the name of the township the building represents during that year. Dr. Rydahl holds a Ph.D. in Theatre History (East Saginaw; Michigan), and taught in that field for 36 years at the University of Iowa, Eastern Illinois, and Central Michigan University. Because of this background, Harriet Olson requested that Rydahl write and direct the historical plays, and produce a CD of the history of each township. The plays demonstrate how town halls were used for voting, political meetings, weddings and community gatherings. The town crier would ring a bell to announce the opening of the polls for voting.

The August 3, 1991 edition of Greenville's newspaper, *The Daily News*, opens with a front page article titled, "Heritage Gets Extra Attention at Festival." It states:

> **SIDNEY** – The Sidney Township Board Friday paid $6 in damages to a farmer whose sheep were killed by a dog, agreed to try and remove stumps from roads and decided to have wooden voting booths built for an upcoming election.
>
> If these items sound less like current issues facing the township and more like they may have been dealt with a century ago, there's a good reason.
>
> Three members of the township's current board re-enacted a township meeting from the late 1800s as part of the Montcalm

Heritage Village celebration, which continues today on the Montcalm Community College campus.

Current Township Treasurer Madalene Jorgensen played the part of past Treasurer Anthony Courter, Trustee Bill Freed acted as Supervisor Charles Wood and Clerk Wesley Thomsen played the part of Clerk Leroy Starks.

The trio used minutes of an actual 1890 meeting as they performed for a crowd of about 50 people packed into the old Sidney Townshp Hall. The hall was built about 1888, and in 1989 it was moved to its present site at Heritage Village, just north of Sidney Road. The players rang a bell announcing the meeting, brightened the hall with an oil lamp and dressed in the garb of the times.

The re-enactment was a new addition to the three-day Heritage Village celebration, and organizers are planning to have a different township host the make-believe meetings each year.

"We can do this for 20 years without having to go back to the beginning,' said Harriet Olson, a member of the Heritage Village Facilities Committee. 'It was Sidney Township's hall, so we thought they should have the first meeting. I think they did great."

Several members of the audience were descendents of those who helped establish Sidney Township in 1857. Those people and their families were recognized with certificates following the meeting.

The make-believe board took action on several issues that the township board addressed over a century ago, including agreeing to build two voting booths at the overwhelming cost of $15.

"Fifteen dollars," exclaimed Clerk Starks, "Do we have that much money in the treasury?"

"I think we have enough to cover it," replied Treasurer Courter. "And what of spending $500 to $600 on road repairs?"

"Whoa, you're talking big money tonight!" Starks said.

Today's Heritage Village activities begin at 10 a.m., continue through 3 p.m., and include parades, folk music and a variety of other special events. (Meyers 1-2)

An actual script of that early play has been preserved in the Sidney Town Hall Scrapbook. The following are brief excerpts:

TOWN MEETING – AUGUST 2, 1991

DATE – SOMETIME IN THE YEAR OF 1890

PLACE – SIDNEY TOWN HALL

CALL TO ORDER – SUPERVISOR GOES TO THE OUTSIDE DOOR AND RINGS HANDBELL AND SAYS: HEAR YE! HEAR YE!! THE TOWN MEETING OF SIDNEY TOWNSHIP IS NOW READY TO BE CALLED TO ORDER.

(TOWNSHIP OFFICIALS TAKE PLACES AT FRONT TABLE) …

DOG DAMAGE REPORT:

I the undersigned, one of the Justices of the Peace of the Township of Sidney in the County of Montcalm do hereby certify that upon the application of John Sibert of said township, the owner of sheep and lambs alleged to have been killed by dog or dogs. I did on the 2nd day of June 1890 proceed to inquire into the matter and to view the sheep and lambs killed and wounded and that I am satisfied that the sheep and lambs belonging to the said John Sibert were killed and wounded by a dog or dogs and in no other manner and that the damages sustained by the said John Sibert by reason of the killing and wounding of the said sheep and lambs is six dollars and I hereby certify that I am not interested in the matter and am not a kin to said John Sibert and that I am not a member of the township board and that my fees for performing said duty amount is $2.00. Given by my hand this 2nd day of June AD 1890. George Holland, Justice of the Peace.

REPORT ON USE OF HALL

Moved and supported that the boys who have made application be allowed to use the town house for an entertainment on condition that they clean the house. Carried. Move that this meeting be adjourned. The clerk will now make some awards to some of the people who are descendents of some of these pioneer families. Composed by Harriet Olson, 1991, based on early minutes. (Sidney II:10)

The Certificate of Appreciation was awarded to each of the following "in grateful recognition of the commitment and dedication of your family to help establish Sidney Township. Through the involvement of your family, you have helped make Sidney Township a more caring community and a homeland of which we can be proud. Montcalm Heritage Village Committee recognizes this dedication" (Sidney II:9). Each of these were dated August 2, 1991, and signed by Jean Brundage, Montcalm Heritage Village Chairperson. The recipients were:

Ruth Jensen	Laverne Noah	Marion Hunsicker	Ana Larsen
Cecile Thomas	Frank Drews	Burl Drews	Bill Courter
Ruth Elaine Burkey	Lemoine White	Jan Pearl	Julie Hopkins
Kay King	Alice Steffins	Morris Hansen	Pearl La Clear
Bank of Sidney			

Over the next twenty years and according to plan, a play featured a different township during each Festival. The final township of Richland was represented in August of 2010 by a special presentation written and produced by Dr. Rydahl with the assistance of Dr. Springsteen. Rydahl began the meeting by announcing, "Welcome to the Town Hall at Heritage Village for our celebration of Richland Township. Richland Township is the 20th and the last township to be organized in Montcalm County" (Richland Township Scrapbook, p. 10.) Visiting dignitaries for the occasion included the current Richland Township board members, head librarian, fire chief, and representative of the Wolverine Power Cooperative. Emphasis was given to early events in Richland's history, and today's Richland Township schools. Committee members hailed the event as a fitting conclusion to the cycle of special presentations. Appropriately, Sidney Township is once again being featured, during the twenty-fifth anniversary year of Heritage Village.

Today, Vivian Hey serves as both the docent and caretaker for the Town Hall. Vivian Hey recounts, "It was 2003 when Harriet Olson asked me to assist her in the Township Hall, and I've enjoyed working it ever since. I love the displayed American flag with 48 stars, pictures of the original county courthouse, scrapbooks from each township in the county, old map of the United States, voting booths, heating stove, and the first ballot box of Sidney Township, originally a cheese box!" (Hey letter).

Here is a picture of downtown Sidney in 1961, with Sidney Road running east and west, and Derby Road running north and south. Notice the old Sidney Town Hall just south of the Church, and north of the Sidney State Bank parking lot. This is the location from which it was moved to Heritage Village. (Photo courtesy of Jim Paris, President of Sidney State Bank)

The Sidney General Store is seen here being towed on a flat-bed trailer during the two-plus mile journey to its new home at Heritage Village in 1989. (Photo courtesy of Maxine Harris)

3.

SIDNEY GENERAL STORE AND THORLAND ICE HOUSE

Sidney General Store

The old country store was donated by Earl (Chris) and Mary Beth Christiansen in 1989. He inherited the building and wanted to preserve its Sidney heritage. This structure was built by Lem and Charles Fish around 1908, and actually served as Sidney's General Store for many years. The Fish family owned and operated the store for some time and lived in the upstairs apartment. Jody Hedrick, MCC's Publications Coordinator and Graphic Designer, is the granddaughter of Lem and Charles Fish, and remembers her mother speaking of growing up as a child in the store's upstairs apartment. She quotes her mother as saying, "There were actually five stores located in downtown Sidney at one time – the Sidney General Store where I served as a 'soda jerk' [soda clerk], a hardware store on the corner that looked very much like the General Store, a drug store (south of the bar), another grocery store, and Petersen's Store" (Hedrick).

At first, the store was red, but Jean Brundage decided to paint it yellow so that it could be clearly seen from Sidney Road. Ironically, the view of the store is today somewhat obscured by several pine trees that had been planted by a local Boy Scout troop. Their intent was to grow the seedlings into small trees that could be planted throughout the village. Unfortunately, the transplanting never occurred. The other pine trees in the village today were planted by Frank Reeder, former MCC Director of Facilities. They had been purchased as small plants for the college graduation, and it was Frank's idea to transplant them throughout the village following commencement.

Jean Brundage appointed herself to be the volunteer and docent in charge of the store, and describes the beginning of its acquisition for the village:

> The store was also moved on a big flatbed truck from its prior location across the street from the Sidney Supper Club ("Just Hangin' Around" Bar and Grill) on Derby Road, just south of Sidney Road. It was completely empty when they gave it to us. Some of the people who used to live in it after the Fish family were not very kind to it. It had tin sides and tin ceilings. We want to replace those sometime. We do have lights for which we're thankful. It's the biggest building in the village. It was somewhat like a Meijer's Store of yesteryear with everything in it – food, clothes, stationery, dry goods, sporting goods, and candy for the children. And since many old country stores also housed the town Post Office, we bought an old original post office from another couple and installed it into this store as well. The cases and items behind the Post Office boxes and counter were donated by some kind folks from Cedar Springs. We bought other shelves from a store in Stanton. People have donated a lot over the years, and we now have a full store. When we have tours, they stop at the first counter and we tell them about that side of the store, then route them around the store and other side. And if they're good, they stop again at the front counter for penny candy. Tours of the whole village take about two and a half hours today, and a good 20 minutes of that are spent in the store. I have been the store keeper since the beginning, which now makes nearly 25 years. Marge Waldron also helps me, and we so enjoy these wonderful experiences with the school children and people of the community. (Brundage interview)

Lillian Christophersen remembers selling baked goods in the Sidney General Store when it was still in operation, at the request of Edith Fish who owned the store and lived in the upstairs apartment at the time. Occasionally, she also took her own card table to the store on which to sell hats. Through these connections, Lillian became involved in the Village and joined the committee.

Interestingly, "William H. Noah established the first store in Sidney, in his house, with money saved from being a soldier in the Civil War, and with a hundred dollars he bought groceries at Ionia and brought them to his cabin" (Olson, *North Sidney* 47). The Sidney General Store at Heritage Village celebrates those early endeavors that helped give rise to the community.

Thorland Ice House

The Thorland Ice House was built by Stan and Irvin Jorgensen between 1923 and 1928, and was located on the family farm near Greenville. The farm was later sold to the Thorlands, who donated it to the Village in 1992. When it was moved to the village, it was placed directly behind the General Store at the request of Brundage and the committee. Brundage recalls,

> When John Thorland gave us the Ice House, we only had four buildings at Heritage Village. This building he gave us was a two story ice house that reminded me of the big ice house my parents had behind their house. Everyone had an ice house back in those days, since you didn't have electricity. The job of the kids was to cut ice blocks out of the lakes and transport them to the ice house and put saw dust in between them. We now use this building during the year to store items for the flea market. (Brundage interview)

Side entrance of the Sidney General Store, with Thorland Ice House in background. Young guests enter the General Store during Festival.

Kathern Hansen waits on a customer while Jean Brundage and Marge Waldron attend to others.

Jean Brundage catches a breather between visiting school groups.

Judy White prepares to greet new guests. Entrance to General Store on Main Street.

The Tool Shed with its "Lean-To" at Heritage Village house
and display a variety of farming tools and equipment.

Among the articles are a horse-drawn sleigh, and field implements.

Many of these implements were donated to the
village by Committee member Dale White.

An old-fashioned "stumping machine" stands behind the Tool Shed.

4.

TOOL SHED AND STUMPING MACHINE

Tool Shed

In 1992, the committee decided the Village needed a tool shed. Clarence and Harriet Olsen (who volunteered at the Town Hall) owned and operated a large dairy farm, and donated the money for the construction of a shed that would be a replica of one of their own. Committee member Fred Ehle built the shed and took ownership of it for several years. More recently, Dale White and other volunteers added a lean-to on the south side of the tool shed. Both the shed and lean-to are now filled with various tools and old implements that were once used in the farming industry. Earl Buskirk serves as today's volunteer in charge of the Tool Shed.

Stumping Machine

The large Stumping Machine was donated to Heritage Village by Howard Petersen of nearby Trufant in 1992, and placed directly behind the Tool Shed. It is a steelyard machine that pulled stumps by means of pulleys and a cable fastened to the tripod of large poles. A team of horses or a yoke of oxen provided the power to pull the stumps. Sidney Lutheran Church gave the stumps that rest beneath the machine. A number of stumps also line the path between the MCC Foundation Farmhouse and the parking lot shared by Heritage Village and Montcalm Community College. An old newspaper article explaining the use of stumping machines may be found on the east wall inside the Edmore Jail:

Old-Time Stump Puller is Michigan Landmark

Tourists driving north through Michigan on U. S. 131 in Montcalm County may wonder what the odd looking machine is that stands by the roadside south of Pierson. It has a triangle of three legs, with cables, pulleys, and a heavy lever.

It is a stump puller and is a successor to the screw-type puller that was used for many years to pull pine stumps.

The chains hanging on the lever were placed underneath the stump through holds dug under the roots. If the soul was sandy, the digging was easy. If it was clay, it was harder work.

With the holes dug, the chains were placed and attached to the heavy metal lever. Notice the cable that is fastened to the leg at the left. It goes up through the three block pulleys and is attached to the lever, which is as near the top of the stump as is possible.

Horses pulled on the end of the cable, raising the lever and the stump with it. Sometimes a second setting had to be made to get the stump out of the ground. The cable-and-lever method was much faster than the screw-type pulling.

After World War I, surplus explosives like TNT and picric acid were made available. Most of the pine stumps had been pulled, but hardwood lands that were being cleared had many stumps blown out of the ground with these explosives. (Anonymous)

C. H. Wendell explains, "Whenever there was new ground to be cleared for farming, the age-old problem of removing the stumps reared its ugly head. In many cases, the larger ones were left to rot away, but this took many years. By the 1850s, a few manufacturers were devising stump pullers to achieve this task" (Wendell 393). One manufacturer, A. B. Farquhar of York, Pennsylvania quoted the famous saying of Archimedes, "Give me a place for my fulcrum, and I will move the world" (Wendell 393).

The Edmore Jail stands on Main Street of Heritage Village.

Items in the Jail House include an old pea-coal stove
and pump organ used as the Sheriff's desk.

Two cells can be seen in the Edmore Jail today...

Occupied by two mannequin inmates!

5.

EDMORE JAIL

Heritage Village continued to grow. A town jail came from Edmore, Michigan, delivered on a trailer that was provided by association volunteers. The Edmore Jail had been used in the 1800s, and was donated to the Village by the town of Edmore in 1992. During the lumbering days it was used mostly to hold boisterous drunks (like Otis on *The Andy Griffith Show*). When sober, they would return to the saloons and repeat the cycle until their money was gone. The following inscription hangs inside the old jail today:

OLD EDMORE JAIL
Submitted by: Mrs. Irene Wagar
"In the old days it cost $9.60, and then some to get drunk. The boisterous drunks were hauled off to jail, then turned loose in the saloons to get drunk again, and back and forth between the jail and the saloon they'd shuttle until their money gave out, then finally they were bedded down behind bars. This jail – its barred windows can still be seen in back of Curtis Hardware – was packed like sardines with lawbreakers. And it was a place where huge rats flourished.

"The city fathers decided one day that a curfew should go into effect to help curb mischievous boys. But what proved to be a more effective curb to their high spirits was the day a jail inmate hung himself by his suspenders. It was a horrible sight to see – him hanging there, swinging back and forth in the wind. He stayed there quite a time until the coroner's arrival from Stanton. Roads were sand trails then, and it took quite awhile for someone to fetch the coroner. So the town's marshal's threat to put a bad boy in jail worked amazingly well for awhile."

Taken from an article written by Shirley Mair when she and her husband, Bruce owned the Edmore Times. Her source of information was Norm Lowford, an Edmore barber, whose parents came to Edmore in 1877-78.

Today, the old Edmore Jail has two cells. Jean Brundage tells how she visited Sauder Village in Archbold, Ohio, and took pictures of the cells in the jail there. She then showed them to her volunteers who designed and created the cells accordingly. These cells are now inhabited by "jail mate mannequins." Brundage recalls that one year a little boy came to her with his dad who said the boy was afraid to go into the jail because of the mannequins. He thought they were real prisoners! Jean told the boy, "Come with me," and led the youngster and his dad to the jail and into one of the cells. She had just put the "dummies" together with salvaged clothes of her husband's. First, she took off the boots, then the shirt, and then the head. The little boy responded, "I knew it wasn't real all the time" (Brundage letter).

But the jailbird "dummies" are not the only items to see in the jail house today. The visitor will also see an old stove, sheriff's uniform, rifle, Billy club, chairs, and several other articles of furniture. In the cabinet next to the cells, one will see a variety of items, including a whisk broom, metal cups and plates, towels, and jail clothes. Beside the cabinet is a crude table with two metal wash basins, a shaving cup and brush, soap, and a hand towel. Beneath it, one notices an old crock pot and bucket on floor. By the wall opposite the cells is what looks at first like the sheriff's desk. But on more careful examination, the item is clearly an old-fashioned pump organ. A sign above the organ reads:

THIS FOLDING PUMP ORGAN
WAS
PLAYED FOR FRIDAY NIGHT
STREET MEETINGS IN SIDNEY
AND
AT THE STANTON JAIL ON
SUNDAY AFTERNOONS
IN

THE LATE NINETEEN THIRTIES AND EARLY FORTIES IT WAS OWNED BY EJNAR C. ANDERSEN OF SIDNEY TOWNSHIP
DONATED BY HIS DAUGHTER ANNA ELIZABETH (BETTY) ANDERSEN HART

Today, the pump organ is in closed position, with a "clerk's desk organizer" on top, and also holds books of county records. This sign above is only one of several documents displayed in the jail. Another is an eye-opening list of auction items from the mid-1800s. Although it is from Kentucky, it was brought to the area by a resident of neighboring Ionia County, Michigan. It reads:

AUCTION SALE
HAVING SOLD MY FARM AND AM LEAVING FOR OREGON TERRITORY BY OX TEAM WILL OFFER ON
March 1, 1842

All ox teams except two teams: Buck and Ben and Tom and Jerry

2 milk cows, 1 grey mare and colt

1 baby yoke, 2 ox carts

1 iron plow with wood mold board

800 feet of poplar weather boards

1,500 ten-foot fence rails

1 sixty gallon soap kettle

85 sugar thoughs made of white ash timber

10 gallons maple syrup

2 spinning wheels

30 pounds of mutton tallow

1 large loom made by Jerry Wilson

300 hoop pones, 100 split hoops

1 32-gallon barrel of Johnson whiskey, 7 years old

100 empty barrels

20 gallons of apple brandy

40 gallons of corn brandy

Oak tan leather, 1 handle hooks

3 scyths. 1 dozen wooden pitch forks

One-half interest in tan-yard

1 32 caliber rifle bullet mold and powder horn

Rifle made by Ben Miller

50 gallons of soft soap, hams, backon [sic] and lard, 10 gallons of sorghum molasses

6 head of Fox Hounds all soft mouthed except one

At the same time will sell my six negro slaves:

2 men 35 and 50 years old, 2 boys, Mulatto wenches, 40 and 30 years old.

Will sell all together to same party as will not separate them

TERMS OF SALE – Cash in hand, or note to draw 4 per cent interest with Clyde Maxwell as security.

My home is two miles south of Versailles, Kentucky on McCoon's Ferry Pile. Sale will begin at 3 a.m. – Plenty of eats and drinks. – Ray Wineland.

Compliments of JOHN H. SCHLOSSER
R. F. D. No 2
IONIA, MICH.
What you want – we have it!

Odd as it may seem to have this hanging in the Edmore Jail, it is a reminder that the jail was also a public establishment. Again, one might think of the jail house on *The Andy Griffin Show*. Other notices on display seem more fitting with the jail itself. One of those is a list of the acting sheriffs of Montcalm County. Here is the list exactly as it is displayed:

SHERIF'S [sic] OF MONTCALM COUNTY

The first sheriff of Montcalm County was Hiram Amsbury.

1891-92	Newton A. Porter
1893-94	Charles M. King
1895-96	Charles M. King

1897-1900	No record
1901-02	Elliot Bellows
1903-04	same
1905-06	Wesley Gaffield
1907-08	No record
1909-10	Alphonsus E. Ward
1911-12	Same
1913-14	Wm. E. Rasmussen
1915-16	same
1917-18	James M. Ford
1921-22	Fred Curtis
1923-24	Fred Curtis
1925-26	Franklin B. Henkel
1927-28	M. Henkel
1929-30	
1931-32	Francis M. Waldo
1933-34	same
1935-42	Chris Hansen
1943-50	Walter H. Arntz
1951-68	Elton Sampson
1969	Thomas Barnwell

Interestingly, Thomas Barnwell's son, William Barnwell, is now serving as the Sheriff in that office. William says he was literally "raised" in the County Jail, much like Opie in the TV series.

And, of course, a visitor to the Edmore Jail will see cell keys. Above a set of encased keys on the north wall is a sign which reads:

ORIGINAL KEYS FROM
THE MONTCALM COUNTY JAIL
ON COURT STREET
DONATED BY FREDA H. GRUNWALD

But as one leaves the jail at Heritage Village, he or she will now notice the hand-carved wooden key fashioned by Phil Frisbie (as he did for most of the Village buildings). Today's "jail-keeper" is Lou Kitchenmaster.

6.

TREBIAN ORCHARD, GARDENS, ENTRANCE, CEMETERY, AND FARM MACHINE SHED (GIFT SHOP)

In 1970, the Montcalm Community College campus had a couple buildings, but no trees. It was stark. When Heritage Village started, it was still just grass land. According to Brundage, "At first, this was just one big field with nothing in it. Then came the early Village buildings. Then, one young girl suggested during a tour that we need more trees and flowers, and so we asked the Master Gardeners to help us out" (Brundage interview).

Trebian Orchard

"That is yet another feature that was enhanced even on the college campus because of the village," Don Burns recalls (Burns). In 1993, Orville Trebian planted several trees on campus and in Heritage Village, to make it more like a real village with shade in the summer time. Early pioneers in Montcalm County planted apple trees, lilac bushes and gardens as soon as they were settled. These growing trees and the ongoing relationship with the Master Gardeners continue to enhance the overall appearance of the Village.

Gardens and Entrance

During this same time period, the idea of flower gardens and a main entrance to the Village also emerged. Tom Learmont reflects:

> We had no real plan for how the village would grow, so a number of years ago I, working with Jean and Edna, developed a master plan showing the possible placement of built facilities and suggested

locations for new additions. Shortly thereafter, the Master Gardeners started to become involved in the Village and as a part of their class they wanted to develop a master plan for flower gardens in the Village. We gave them the drawing I had made, which they modified by adding their suggested plans for trees and flower gardens. One item they added was an entrance which had as it focal point a stone wall on each side of the entrance driveway. Knowing that most likely it would never get built, I conceived of the idea of making the picket type fence entrance that you see today. I made a drawing of the concept, developed a cost estimate and presented it to both Jean and the Master Gardeners. They liked the idea and the Master Gardeners said they would pay for the supplies if I would build it. I built it and they did the gardens—thus the history on the entrance. (Learmont interview)

Flora Phelps remembers her start at Heritage Village working as a Master Gardener. She shares, "I first became involved at the Village in 1995. As I am a Master Gardener, Mary and Carlton Ferguson asked me if I'd help with putting in antique roses from Grand Rapids. Max and I helped them put them in and cover them with necessary bedding for the winter in 1996" (Phelps).

In addition to the many flower beds of the Village, one will also see today "The Herb Garden at Heritage Village," located just north of the Shoen Log House. A plaque inside the Log House explains the uses for many of these herbs:

The Herb Garden at Heritage Village

The family living in the Log Cabin in the 1800s would have likely grown some herbs to use in various ways. The herb garden on the north side of the cabin includes some of the herbs they might have grown. The following gives some examples of how they may have used them for culinary, medicinal and ornamental purposes.

Sage – *Salvnia officinalis*: Used to flavor meats, stuffing, breads and sausages. Sage was also used to repel insects especially flies and cabbage moths. The plant makes a good border contrast to flowers like orange lilies and roses the family might have grown. The variety here is Burgarden Sage.

Chives – *Sllium schoenoprasum:* The most common use of chives is in cooking. They taste like sweet mild onions and would have been chopped in many recipes. In the spring the purple blossoms can be eaten. Chives could be easily tied in bundles and hung to dry for winter use.

Garlic Chive – *Allium tuberosum:* These were used much like regular chives but they have a garlic flavor rather than an onion flavor. They have flat leaves rather than round and the white flowers appear late in the summer.

Comfrey – *Symphytum officianal:* This large leaf plant was used mostly for medicine. The leaves can be chopped and mashed to rub on as a medicine for skin diseases and to help bruises heal. The family in the log cabin may have made comfrey tea but it has since been found that this is not safe and may cause cancer.

Thyme – *Thymus vulgaris:* Thyme would have been used by the family in cooking to flavor all kinds of meat as well as almost all vegetables and mushroom.

Mint – *Mentha:* This may have been a favorite because it grows easily and spreads quickly, but more importantly, it has many uses. As a medicine mint tea tastes good and cured indigestion, upset stomach and colic. In cooking, the family could make mint jelly and candy and add extra taste to meats and vegetables like carrots or new potatoes.

Other herbs planted in the garden include bee balm, dill, lemon balm, lavender, and Chamomile.

Village Cemetery

The Village Cemetery was made in 1994 as a memorial to pioneers. The stump fence at the back of the plot is made of roots of the white pine trees that once grew here. The "foot stone" marker was used to mark the foot of the grave. Obviously, there is no one buried here. Tombstones for the cemetery were either acquired or donated because they were replaced by newer stones for departed loved ones. However, an interesting story surrounds the tallest tombstone in this small plot located beside the Town Hall. Beneath a beautifully sculpted rose relief it reads, "Hannah G. – Wife of C. R. Dickinson – Died Mar. 10, 1866: Aged 31 years, 9 mos. 12 days." An interesting folklore of the Village is that a man was removing the top stone step leading to the back porch on his house in a nearby community, and turned it over in great surprise to discover it was this tombstone! Not knowing what else to do with it, he donated it to Heritage Village. Later, when committee member Gary Hauck was giving a tour of Heritage Village in 2009, a gentleman looked at the tombstone and said, "That was my great grandmother! I wondered whatever happened to the old stone when the family replaced it. I'm glad it found a home here."

One other special feature of the cemetery is the rose bush that grows in its very center, and is protected by a surrounding wire screen. This bush is a descendant of a rose bush at Andersonville Prison Camp during the Civil War. Andersonville Prison Camp is officially known as Camp Sumter, and served as a Confederate Prisoner-of-war camp in Georgia. The bush was brought to Montcalm County by a descendent of one who was in the prison camp during the Civil War. A sign now marks this feature, donated by the Keith McInnis Family in 2010.

Farm Machine Shed (Gift Shop)

A Farm Machine Shed was built by volunteers in 1994, and has served as the Heritage Village Gift Shop. It is also used for storage, and has recently housed an old fire engine from Crystal, Michigan as well. Crystal Fire Chief Bob Brundage was instrumental in the acquisition, which was a gift of Crystal Township. Tom Learmont fondly recalls working on this building:

My wife Ruth and I painted the green building which we call the Gift Shop. We enjoyed working together. One thing which is most memorable on that project was while we were painting, I was up on a ladder and Ruth was working at ground level. Just then Ivan, our member who often cuts the grass, came around with his weed—whacker and cut right next to the building and covered the wet paint with grass clippings! Ruth sure was upset with him and refused to do any more painting! To this day she has not forgiven him. (Learmont interview)

The bright red Caboose of the Village can be entered and explored. It served as an office and bedroom for those who operated the train.

The Water Tower and Handcar House were added later, as well as the Depot and Steam Engine.

7.

CABOOSE, WATER TOWER, AND MAINTENANCE OF WAY HANDCAR HOUSE

The Caboose

The Caboose was originally owned by the Chesapeake & Ohio Railroad. The company donated it to the Montcalm Intermediate School District who, in turn, donated it to Heritage Village. It was moved to the Village in 1995 by West Shore Service, Inc. movers. Based on its design, it is believed to have been built about 1915.

Bob Brundage, husband of Jean Brundage, was the leader in setting up the rails and coordinating the movement of the caboose to the Village (Brundage communication). The caboose was first located where the steam engine is now. It was in poor condition at that time as several windows were broken, most of the roofing was blown off, some of the remaining roof boards were rotted and water was destroying the interior. The C & O Railroad, while still in its ownership, had covered the outside of the caboose with plywood and steel strapping covered the joints between the sheets of plywood. It was at that time painted yellow. Jean Brundage asked Tom Learmont if he would like that unit as his building, which he accepted. Being somewhat new to the Village and not having had any leadership roles as yet in the operation, he looked over the unit and prepared a paper on what he thought should be accomplished first. He made a series of sketches, listed the items needing to be repaired or replaced, and developed a cost estimate of about $350. The first effort was to repair the roof, replace the broken windows, install a door, and build steps leading to the two ends of the caboose, making it more accessible. He presented the paper to the committee during a monthly meeting and asked for approval to proceed. This was granted, and thus began Learmont's first project in the Village in which he took a leadership role (Learmont letter). Valgeen Mack assisted with the work on the Caboose interior (Mrs. Mack letter).

The Caboose served as a moving office for the conductor, a lookout observation platform to see the train ahead, and a limited maintenance shop. It also served as the onboard maintenance crew's quarters. The conductors on freight trains were responsible for keeping records of what cars made up the train, where they were going, where they needed to be dropped off and where along the route cars were to be added or picked up. Every car had a number that the conductor used for recording purposes. He had to assure that an accurate record was maintained of the official numerals on the cars of his train, which he either dropped off or picked up along the route. This information was then passed onto the different station masters as the train proceeded. This was the national integrated system of tracking all railroads that ran throughout the country (Learmont letter).

Sitting at his desk in the Caboose office, the conductor maintained all of that information using a piece of paper and stubby pencil. Today, each railroad car has a computer chip in it, and can be tracked from a satellite with the car's locations being tracked by computer. Two men would sit in the cupola of the caboose, one on either side, looking forward as the train moved down the track. They were to observe anything that might occur along the way which could pose a problem, such as people trying to get a free ride, a brake that was dragging, or a wheel bearing that was overheating. They could then inform the conductor or engineer of the situation before a disaster would happen. Dragging brakes or the overheating of a wheel bearing was indicated by smoke, sparks or flames appearing from one of the cars. When the train was stopped, the maintenance men in the caboose would then add grease to the wheel bearing boxes to eliminate the overheating problem or manually repair the dragging brake shoe. With the invention of sealed bearings and improved brake design, the need for such observation and on-the-track repairs were reduced to the point that onboard maintenance crews were no longer needed. Since maintenance men and the conductor spent long hours riding in the caboose, bunks were added to provide a place to sleep during off duty hours (Learmont letter).

Provisions were also made for cooking some meals. The toilet facilities were nothing more than a toilet which dropped right on to the railroad right-of-way. There were, for the most part, no holding tanks. The crew kept some tools, grease, flares and other emergency supplies in the caboose at all times. Caboose and other rail cars operated in a less-than-safe environment due to weather, vibration, and humping and were required to be structurally strong. The design of the caboose of this age is somewhat unique as the framework for the sides and roof were all made of 3"x3" by ½" thick angle iron, to which 4'x4' wooden timbers were bolted. The roof siding and interior paneling were then nailed to the wooden timbers. All interior doors had strong latches. Steel rods were installed to hold the stove segments together and to bolt them to the floor to avoid tipping over while humping or traveling down the track. Later model cabooses were made of an all-welded steel construction including the siding (Learmont letter).

Periodically over the past 10 years, Learmont along with other volunteers have made additional repairs to the caboose. Learmont recounts:

> The old siding was removed and replaced with the original type "car-siding." Window frames were rebuilt, and the interior doors were fixed. The interior was painted gray and the exterior was painted the current bright red. A number of additional repairs are still required. The caboose was moved to its current location when the steam engine and tender arrived. I had no involvement with the moving of the caboose or of the setting of the steam engine or tender. My involvement with the caboose has been off and on as others took it over. I still hope to someday get back to completing the restoration. (Learmont letter)

For many years, Ruth Hansen has given tours of the Caboose. Today, Larry Beard is the volunteer in charge of the Caboose.

Water Tower

The Heritage Village Water Tower takes its place near the Caboose and the Town Hall. It was dismantled from its original location in Sheridan and reconstructed at the Village. Instructor Larry Yaw and students from the Montcalm Career Center welding class rebuilt it and set the base in 1995.

Water towers were placed near rail tracks and supplied water for the train steam engines.

Maintenance of Way Handcar House

Built by Dale White and other volunteers in 2003, the Maintenance of Way Handcar House, also called a section shed, housed motorized handcars (speeders), regular handcars, and trailers. The long-tongued trailers hauled rail sections and equipment for repairs. Section workers (gandy-dancers) stored their spike hammers, wrenches, other tools, and fuel in the M-O-W. It is located just south of the McBride's Depot.

Exterior of Rush Dairy. Elle Kemph serves ice cream to a young guest during Festival. Alvin and Margaret Rush explain the use of the bottling machine. Interior of Dairy with Soda Fountain and equipment.

8.

RUSH DAIRY

The Rush Dairy was located in Sheridan as well. The milk bottling equipment was donated by Alvin and Margaret Rush of the original Rush Dairy. The Veteran's Memorial Fund Committee donated the funds for the material for the building, which was built by volunteers in 1995. Alvin, himself, sawed all of the lumber for this construction at his own sawmill. Years ago, milk was bottled and then delivered by horse and wagon to town customers. Alvin and Margaret still maintain the dairy as members of the Heritage Village Committee, and serve ice cream on parlor-like tables and chairs during the Annual Heritage Festival.

Rush and Sons Dairy was in Alvin's family. He explains, "My dad started the dairy and all us boys had to work on the farm with the dairy cattle and in the processing plant for the pasteurized milk bottling which was the mainstay of the business" (A. Rush). A history of the building can be found on a poster in the Rush Dairy building. It reads:

1935 – Walter Rush started Rush Dairy, bottled fresh milk in pint and quart glass jars. They delivered milk to the Sheridan area.

1938 – Bought Witter's in Stanton.

1940 – Milking 50 cows now. Started delivery to Crystal, bought a pasteurizer and steam boiler from Carnation Creamery (which used to be in Sheridan, Michigan) for $1100.00.

1942 – Started pasteurizing milk. Harders helped build the milk house.

1945 – Changed the name to Rush and Sons Dairy. Started buying milk

55

from local farms: Regis, May, Beardslee and Reese, and Fosburg. Started deliveries to Greenville and began to process chocolate milk.

1948 – Started deliveries to Gibson Refrigerator Company in Greenville, Michigan. Mr. Rush delivered to co-workers there in ½ pint bottles.

1950 – Started delivering to stores; LaSalles and Sayers in Crystal. Also started deliveries to the Crystal Palladium Bowling Alley. Bought cottage cheese and butter from Amble Creamery and delivered along with milk.

1951 – Fire destroyed the barn and all animals.

1961 – Rush and Sons Dairy closed, ending an era of milk deliveries to the door.

Alvin Rush continues to explain:

I initiated the Rush Dairy building as a way of showing others how milk was pasteurized and bottled. The equipment is what I could salvage from my dad's processing plant. My dad did not realize the importance of saving much of the equipment and many bottles and caps were destroyed. Today, he would be proud of the legacy he leaves behind of a bygone era. Likewise, I am proud that my family's business can be used as a history tool for those who've never seen how milk is processed and bottled. (A. Rush)

Sometime after the installation of the Rush Dairy, Jesse and Marilyn Fox conceived of the idea of having an ice cream shop with a soda fountain in the dairy as well. They were able to find donors of ice cream tables and chairs, and helped move them into the dairy. Jesse and Marilyn have also assisted Alvin and Margaret as docents in the Rush Dairy.

On the upper left, the McBride's Depot can be seen at its original location in McBride, MI. (Photo courtesy of Dale White) At the top right, one can compare the same building on its present location in Heritage Village. The middle photos show the schedule and ticket window, and the lower photos picture the waiting area, and the interior of the office.

9.

MCBRIDE'S DEPOT

McBride's Depot

The McBride's Depot was located in McBride, Michigan, when Frank and June Parr donated the depot, and funded its move to the Village. The railroad came through the area in 1877 and erected the depot near McBride's Mill on the Detroit, Lansing, and Northern Line. The Pere Marquette ran through McBride for many years. Valgeen Mack was instrumental in acquiring the McBride's Depot for the Village, and Alvin Rush assisted Harriet Olson in getting a mover to transport the Depot from McBride to Heritage Village. Rollaway Movers accomplished the delivery in 1995.

Following the extensive renovation work on the Caboose, Tom Learmont began working on the Depot, and coordinated the efforts of other volunteers who joined him in the project. Like the Caboose, the Depot was also in poor condition when it was acquired by the Village. It originally was set high on several strong posts, and an orange snow fence placed around it for safety purposes. Learmont built a set of steps, which he later moved to the back entrance of the store, fixed the doors and sanded and varnished the floor in the waiting room.

About this same time, Don and Ruth Hansen joined the Association. Don, having been a Railroad Station Manager during his working career, was naturally interested in the Depot and Caboose. Don was a good handyman and a welcomed addition to the Village Committee. Don and Learmont then teamed up to begin what would become about a two-year effort in restoring the Depot. Near the end of this project Don became very ill, but continued as long as possible. His daughter, Nancy, also came out to assist as she enjoyed working with her father. After Don's passing, his daughter still came to the Village to assist with the painting of the depot. She and her husband later returned to paint the Caboose interior as well. Today, Larry Beard is the volunteer in charge of the Depot, as well as the Caboose.

As one mills about in the depot, there are many interesting objects to notice. The waiting area, known as "The Frank Parr, Jr. Room," is complete with benches, and a stack of period luggage in the corner. (Frank Parr, Jr. was the last owner of the Depot and insisted that it be called the McBride's Depot rather than the McBride Depot. Interestingly, a disagreement still exists on the part of many townspeople.) On the walls hang old black and white photographs of the train arriving at the depot, and a giant map of Michigan. An antique water crock and ladle grace one corner, while on the opposite end of the room is a checkerboard resting on a tiny table with two chairs and a nearby spittoon. An old clock and large train lantern are next to the track door, and beside the ticket counter is a small pot-belly stove and cedar chest.

On the counter in the office behind the ticket booth, one will note an authentic paycheck #6691 from the Manistee & Northern Railway Company dated April 30, 1946 and made out to Bernard J. Hansen, ENGR. Beside it rests a Timetable for Passenger Trains 1955-1957 for the lines: Canadian National, Grand Trunk Railway, Canadian Pacific, Erie, Lackawanna, Sante Fe, Illinois Central, Great Northern, Chicago & Eastern, Frisco, Rock Island, Norfolk & Western, and Southern Railway System. Behind the counter are old wooden filing cabinets and two old desks, bearing typewriters and adding machines. For those who lived during this time period, this display is considered amazingly authentic.

10.

PAVILION AND BANDSTAND

The Pavilion

The Pavilion was planned by Fred Ehle and built by the Clark Construction Company in 1998. It was built to provide a sheltered picnic area for visitors to the Village. Dale White and other volunteers more recently built the food booth under the pavilion. In early times, structures like this were enclosed and used for family outings and dances. Miriam Zimmerman is the volunteer in charge of the Pavilion, and also serves as the secretary of the Heritage Village Committee.

The Bandstand

The Bandstand was donated by the Master Gardeners, and built by the Bowen Construction Company in 2000. Most towns had a bandstand in the Village Green, which was a focal point for celebrations and political orations. "In the earlier years, there was a Sidney Band with Robert Courter, Lyndon Noah, and others. Then Frank Mattison came to Sidney and gave lessons to Sidney area young folks. They held band concerts on the lawn… An ice-cream social made it quite a social event" (Olson, *North Sidney* 49). Today, the Bandstand on the Heritage Village "Green" is a gathering place for country music bands and other performers during the Festival.

Elaine Johnson and Flora Phelps initiated the idea of a gazebo, or Bandstand, and provided leadership for the project until its completion. Money was raised by selling plants at the annual plant sale of the Master

Gardeners Association. Today, funds raised by the Master Gardeners' annual plant sale are used for beautification projects and upkeep of the gardens at Heritage Village and throughout Montcalm County.

The Master Gardeners of the Montcalm area are volunteers affiliated with the Michigan State University Extension Program, learning about horticulture through service-learning projects. Under the direction of Vicky Bohn, they continue to maintain the Bandstand and the gardens surrounding it.

The Heritage Village Bandstand and Pavilion grace the Village Green, which serves as the centerpiece. (James Wilcox and Company perform during Festival.) One is led to think of the well-known poem by Jane Taylor, The Village Green:

> "On the cheerful village green,
> Skirted round with houses small,
> All the boys and girls are seen,
> Playing there with hoop and ball.
>
> "Now they frolic hand in hand,
> Making many a merry chain;
> Then they form a warlike band,
> Marching o'er the level plain.
>
> "Now ascends the worsted ball,
> High it rises in the air,
> Or against the cottage wall,
> Up and down it bounces there.
>
> "Then the hoop, with even pace,
> Runs before the merry throngs;
> Joy is seen in every face,
> Joy is heard in cheerful songs.
>
> "Rich array, and mansions proud,
> Gilded toys, and costly fare,
> Would not make the little crowd
> Half so happy as they are.
>
> "Then, contented with my state,
> Where true pleasure may be seen,
> Let me envy not the great,
> On a cheerful village green.

Steam Engine #7456 beside the McBride's Depot at Heritage Village.

11.

STEAM ENGINE #7456

The Steam Switch Engine #7456, class o-18-a, Type 0-6-0, weighing 174,000 pounds was built in 1920 (*Montcalm Heritage Village*). The tender, weighing 130,000 pounds hold 5,500 gallons of water and 9 tons of coal. The engine and tender made their last run in 1950. They were purchased for $41,000 and moved to the Village in 2000 by West Shore Service, Inc.

But the story of how the Village acquired it is quite intriguing. Bob Brundage, Crystal Fire Chief and husband of Heritage Village Chairperson Jean Brundage, went to West Shores Corporation in Coopersville to get supplies for the Fire Department. Surprisingly, the office of this business was in an old passenger train car! During his conversation with company owner Jeff DePidka, Chief Brundage learned that Mr. DePidka had a steam train engine as well. A short time later, a group of Heritage Village members took a trip to Coopersville for a tour of the old Fire Hall. They saw lots of old Fire Department memorabilia, and saw the 1920 Steam Switch Engine. While admiring the engine, Mr. DePidka told Brundage and the others that he would be willing to sell it to Heritage Village for 40,000.00, and they could pay for it in annual installments of $6000.00. When this was completed, Mr. DePidka had his crew bring the Steam Engine on rail to Greenville, and then deliver it by flat-bed truck the rest of the way to Sidney (Brundage communication).

According to Burns:

This was an absolutely huge undertaking – the locomotive project requiring enormous energy! The train locomotive came all the way from Coopersville near Marne, traveling part of the distance by rail, and part of it disassembled on a very large truck. This was an extra big project that took the Village out of its originally intended timeframe. And because all the asbestos had to first be removed from the boiler tank, the cost of the acquisition and move came to over $40,000 dollars. One can only imagine the number of spaghetti dinners and quilt raffles the volunteers conducted in an amazing fundraising endeavor! (Burns)

Larry Beard is the appointed caretaker of the Steam Switch Engine. As docent, he is donned in his engineer's cap and bright red neck scarf when he conducts his tours.

The Doctor's House of Heritage Village is a reminder of Dr. S. Derby,
the first physician to settle in the area who lived in a similar home.
(Derby Lake is named after him.) When not practicing medicine
in his home, "He usually made his rounds on foot, accompanied
by his dog, and carrying a gun" (Olson, North Sidney 46).

12.

DOCTOR'S HOUSE

The Doctor's House and funds to move it were donated by John Bookwalter in honor of Clarence Olson, and it was transported from Stanton in 2000 by the William House Moving Company. A doctor's office is replicated in this home, which was renovated and decorated by volunteers. During pioneer days the doctors often saw patients in their home office or made house calls. Max Phelps, a licensed carpenter who began as a volunteer at the Shoen Log House was asked to remodel the house, build ramps, and make the repairs, along with Dale White, and Jesse and Marilyn Fox. According to Mr. Phelps, "The Doctor's House became my priority because it needed a lot of work and I had the time to do it. It needed major work, and we tried to restore it as close to the original as possible. The doctor's office was put in the front bedroom as a semblance of olden days, and a new chimney was installed in the house" (M. Phelps letter). The committee also asked Jesse and Marilyn Fox to work on the roof, siding, flooring, painting, and wallpapering.

Jean Brundage also recalls doing a lot of work on the Doctor's House, and helping to furnish it. "Many individuals donated items that are in the Doctor's House today," she explains. "The old telephone came from Jim Steere of Crystal; the Sterling Silver pieces on the kitchen shelf and the stove in the living room had belonged to a judge in Edmore, and the coffee grinder was one that Bob and I received from Ada LaDu and we donated it. Committee member Marge Waldron gave us the cradle in the bedroom, living room chair, and the old clock on the wall. The dishes came from Maude Boltz, Bob's grandmother" (J. Brundage communication). The books and toys came from the Brundage household as well. Interestingly, the little folding bed had belonged to Bob Brundage's great grandfather, Oren Sebring, who was a Civil War veteran.

The old organ was in the store for years before being moved into the Doctor's House, and the quilts on the bed were made for the Village by "The Quilters' Quorum of Edmore." The stove in the kitchen belonged to Arvilla Strouse of Butternut, and the tiny refrigerator belonged to docent Vivien Hey. It was Phil Frisbie who donated the settee, or two-person couch, and the old desk came from Dr. Bob Painter. In the doctor's office, the glass case and all of the surgical and doctor's instruments were gifts of Dr. Tom Ferguson DDS of Carson City in memory of his brother and father (both physicians). The scrubs, old fashioned physician's bag, and picture of *The Doctor* were given by Dr. Carl Hansen, "who practiced medicine for over 30 years in Stanton. Dr. Hansen was the husband of Village member Edna Hansen, and was well-liked by the community" (J. Brundage communication). The large picture is a copy of the famous piece by Sir Luke Fildes, which hangs in the National Gallery of London. Resting on the glass case is the Pharmacist's License of Otto Cummings of Stanton, dated July 1, 1921.

Flora Phelps, Max's wife, works the house as today's appointed docent. She reflects:

> The stories surrounding the Doctor's House are interesting for those who are unfamiliar with things like; a doctor making house calls, having his office in his home for those in need who were able to travel to see him, or a neighbor who might come and play on the family pump organ to entertain those waiting to see the doctor. The family parlor became the waiting room. Many don't realize that a doctor might be needed several miles away and in the days of horse and buggy or sleigh, he would drive as far as he could and might have to walk the rest of the way if the weather was too bad, or even have to stop and rest at someone's home, get some warm broth or soup, then continue on to see the patient. Times were very difficult then. (F. Phelps letter)

One very interesting item that Flora always enjoys pointing out to visitors in the Doctor's House is a peg leg—an artificial leg made from wood that was strapped on to enable the person to walk again. This peg leg was donated by a gentleman known as "Peg Leg Brown" of Crystal (Brundage telephone interview).

When not assisting her husband in the Rush Dairy, Margaret Rush assists Flora in the Doctor's House. She writes:

> I'm grateful to be helping Mrs. Phelps with the Doctor's House. Another little tie to it is that when I was in high school and had my very first job in Lyle's Bakery in Stanton, I worked with Eva Gale, the lady who lived in that house in Stanton. I will also note that some kitchen dishes and other items in the Doctor's House are some like we had in our home when I was growing up; there are several dishes that came from boxes of oatmeal, and I still use a Ritz cracker can just like the one in the Doctor's House! (M. Rush letter)

Of special interest to Margaret are these observations while volunteering in the Doctor's House:

> We talk about not having electricity in the early days. One day last year a young boy who was visiting the Doctor's House with his class noticed an electrical outlet in the kitchen. He wanted to know why that was there when we didn't have electricity. Well, it is because it is wired with that one outlet only so that it if is very hot during the Heritage Festival, as it often is, then we can plug in one fan, if needed. That was a very observant young man! Probably the other thing of special interest is the old party line telephone, the likes of which we had when I was a young person living in the country. We didn't have any phone until someone on our road needed one for their work, so they had a phone line run on our road, finally. (M. Rush letter)

At top: Entrican Rural School with the two annexes
that became the Hat Shoppe & Barbershop.

13.

BELLE'S HAT SHOPPE AND DELL'S BARBERSHOP

Belle's Hat Shoppe

Belle's Hat Shoppe was originally an annex to the Entrican Rural School. Geraldine Christensen recounts, "I swept the floor of the Hat Shoppe many times for five years when it was the entry way for the Entrican Rural School where I taught! (G. Christensen letter). It was donated by Gene and Ruby Jeppesen, and moved to the Village in 1998 by volunteers who also renovated and furnished it in 2001. In the Village, the shop is located on the main street, next to the Edmore Jail. Robert Buskirk was one who took the lead in this project. He writes, "The Hat Shoppe was in bad shape when it was moved to the village. It was quite a challenge to put it together and make it useful! It took quite a bit of carpentry work and painting to get it where it looks today." (Buskirk letter). Dale White assisted in the painting of the Hat Shoppe.

Once the Hat Shoppe was moved, repaired, and painted, Jean Brundage asked Marge Waldron if she would like to decorate it and take charge of it. Marge took on that responsibility in addition to assisting Jean at the store. Of particular interest to Waldron is the story of the store's namesake that now hangs on the front door:

Belle Potter's Hat Shoppe

Early in the 1900's, there was a ladies hat shop in Stanton, Michigan, owned by Belle Potter. The shop was located in the same block as the Stanton Hotel with an entrance on Main Street as well as a rear door that opened into the hotel lobby.

One evening during a ladies meeting held at the hotel, the ladies deposited their hats in the cloak room upon arriving. During the meeting, Otto Cummins secretly removed the hats from the cloak room and distributed them among the hats on display in Belle's Hat Shoppe. At the end of the meeting, there was utter confusion as the ladies searched for their hats mixed in with all the new hats.

One hat on display in the Heritage Village "Belle's Hat Shoppe" was purchased in the late 1920's or early 1930's by Reato Frisbie during the auction of the contents of the original Belle Potter Hat Shoppe.

Dell's Barber Shop

Dell's Barber Shop was also an annex to the Entrican Rural School and donated by Ruby and Gene Jeppesen. It was moved to the Village in 2001, renovated and furnished by volunteers in 2002. One can find the small shop beside the Rush Dairy. Dale White helped to move the building, repair and paint it, and set it up as it looks today. Both the Hat Shoppe and Barbershop were special projects for Dale. He explains, "I grew up in Entrican. The buildings that now comprise Belle's Hat Shop and Dell's Barbershop are made from the two annexes of the Entrican Rural School, which I attended for grades 1, 2, and 3" (D. White letter).

Exterior and interior of the Blacksmith Shop. Bill Raymor demonstrates the work of a village blacksmith during the Heritage Festival.

14.

BLACKSMITH SHOP

The Blacksmith Shop was built in 2002 from salvaged lumber from a building originally located in Howard City and donated by Vern and Kyle Crater. Dale White and other volunteers razed the building and rebuilt it as a shop at the Village. It is equipped with a forge, an anvil, and "Smithy" tools. *The Story of North Sidney Area 1884-1984* explains how, "The Blacksmith was an important man in the pioneer community. Many of our early tools and machinery were crafted by blacksmiths in the area. In Sidney, the names of Waldemar Thomsen and James Anderson come to mind. Mike Christensen also worked in Sidney Township as well as in Stanton, [where he was joined by] Ray Piatt, Jack Brooks, John Buckrell, Bert Gale, Ed Brooks, Dale Sherwood, Clyde Cooper, and Pete Rice" (Olson 93). Dressed in his period garb, volunteer docent and association member Bill Raymor demonstrates the work of the blacksmith, reminiscent of Longfellow's famous poem, *The Village Blacksmith*:

Under a spreading chestnut tree
The village smithy stands;
The smith, a mighty man is he,
With large and sinewy hands;
And the muscles of his brawny arms
Are strong as iron bands.
His hair is crisp, and black, and long,
His face is like the tan;

His brow is wet with honest sweat,
He earns whate'er he can,
And looks the whole world in the face,
For he owes not any man.
Week in, week out, from morn till night,
You can hear his bellows blow;
You can hear him swing his heavy sledge,
With measured beat and slow,
Like a sexton ringing the village bell,
When the evening sun is low.
And children coming home from school
Look in at the open door;
They love to see the flaming forge,
And hear the bellows roar,
And catch the burning sparks that fly
Like chaff from a threshing-floor.
He goes on Sunday to the church,
And sits among his boys
He hears the parson pray and preach,
He hears his daughter's voice,
Singing in the village choir,
And it makes his heart rejoice.
It sounds to him like her mother's voice,
Singing in Paradise!
He needs must think of her once more,
How in the grave she lies;
And with his hard, rough hand he wipe
A tear out of his eyes.
Toiling,--rejoicing,--sorrowing,
Onward through life he goes;
Each morning sees some task begin,
Each evening sees it close;
Something attempted, something done,
Has earned a night's repose.
Thanks, thanks to thee, my worthy friend,
For the lesson thou hast taught!

Thus at the flaming forge of life
Our fortunes must be wrought;
Thus on its sounding anvil shaped
Each burning deed and thought!
    (Henry Wadsworth Longfellow)

Exterior and interior of Print Shop. Clyde Pritchard explains
the operation of the old Print Shop during Festival.

15.

PRINT SHOP

The Print Shop is a replica of a small town newspaper office where the local paper was printed. It was built by Dale White and other volunteers in 2003. Early papers provided news, advertising, and other notices such as auction sales. Most of the equipment in the shop was donated by James H. Reid and facilitated by Clyde Pritchard of C & C Printing in Stanton in 2002. Other items on display were given by the Carson City *Gazette,* and by Phil Frisbie.

The old printing press was a stand-alone machine that was usually operated by a hand-pull lever and gears. Tiny letters of metal type were placed into a tray-like frame, creating a "page." By pulling a lever, rollers would be activated to roll over a metal plate of paste ink, and then run over the type in the tray or page-frame. When a piece of paper is sandwiched between the inked letters and the press, the result is the printed page. Earlier renditions of the printing press used a giant screw to press the paper on the type tray. During the 1800s, steam-powered presses were sometimes used. However, most small-town newspapers continued to use a manual press.

The Heritage Village Print Shop is located on Main Street, between the Sidney General Store and Belle's Hat Shoppe. Clyde Pritchard often comes to the Village during Festival, and demonstrates the printing press in operation.

Exterior and interior of the Village Church. Designer & builder Tom Learmont holds the blueprints as he poses with the "town parson," Gary Hauck. Other pictures show the Hauck Wedding, visiting school children, the Story Lady, and Bob Milne at the piano.

16.

VILLAGE CHURCH

The Village Church is a replica of early churches built in the area from the late 1800s to early 1900s. The Brown Construction Company of Carson City began construction of the foundation, framework and roof in the fall of 2004. Volunteers installed the siding, insulation and all the interior finish work. Brooks Electric provided the wiring. The final inspection was done in July of 2005. The first guests of the Village Church on July 20, 2005, were six Red Hatters from the area (Village Church guestbook). To help raise funds for the church, bricks for the short sidewalk at the foot of the church stairs were sold for $100 apiece that could either bear the name of the donor or someone the donor wished to honor. There are 106 engraved bricks as part of that pavement today. Some are memorials, some are to honor local church congregations, some were placed by the Master Gardeners, and others recognize committee members, volunteers, or special events. Tom Learmont took the lead role in the church project. He reflects:

> We wanted a church for the Village but did not find one that we could move. So, it was decided that we would build our own. I took the lead effort in the design and construction of the church. At first, I made a number of different concept drawings and a few models for the group to view. Finally, we arrived at the design of the current church. I made detailed drawings of the proposed building, but the county building department insisted that they be approved by a licensed architect. So, we hired an architect who essentially transferred the information on his drawing and signed them — meeting this county requirement. I

then led the search for a contractor to construct the building. Members of our association then installed the siding on the building, finished the interior and painted it. In addition to me, extensive work was also done by Dale White, Bob Buskirk, Jesse and Marilyn Fox and others to some degree as well. (Learmont interview)

Central among the engraved bricks in the sidewalk is a large square brick with the inscription, "Tom Learmont, The Design and Construction Leader – In Memory of My Father." Jesse Fox laid the brick sidewalk, organized a painting party to paint the exterior of the church, and helped his wife, Marilyn, varnish the interior of the church house, including the wooden ceiling (J. Fox telephone interview).

During the construction of the Village Church, Bob Buskirk heard that three churches in the Six Lakes area were going to merge, and one of the old buildings had been sold to local funeral director and MCC alumnus, Steve Brigham. Interested in acquiring the pews, Buskirk approached Mr. Brigham (Buskirk telephone interview). These facts were confirmed. According to Mr. Brigham, the Asbury United Methodist Church of Lakeview, Six Lakes United Brethren Church, and Belvidere United Methodist Church were merging to form the New Life United Methodist Church of Six Lakes. Brigham purchased the building and pews of the Six Lakes UB Church to use for a funeral home, and only had one congregant interested in having one pew. The pews were only used in the funeral home for a brief period, and Brigham was now interested in selling them. "The pews are over a hundred years old," Brigham explains. "The original church was built in 1892 and burned down in 1920, but the pews were spared. Only one pew had a charred end. I know they were worth quite a bit more, but offered to sell them at $100.00 each. Struggling to start a new business, every bit helped. But when Bob approached me and asked about buying ten for Heritage Village for $1000.00, I decided to donate all the rest" (Brigham telephone interview).

The oak pews are beautifully crafted, with a design on the sides of St. Patrick's (Celtic) cross, surrounded by a sweeping circle of five routed lines interlaced with a diagonally positioned square having four loops embracing the circle. Because of the size of the building and length of the pews, they had to be sawn off on the ends to fit inside the sanctuary. Two of the end pieces were refashioned to use on the platform for the parson and worship leader. With the pews, the church seats 85 guests comfortably. Running down the center aisle between the pews is a lovely runner that was a discarded carpet literally found along the road. It was Marilyn Fox who found the rug, had it cleaned, cut it in half and joined it end to end to make the runner.

Other donated furnishings include an 1880s pump organ donated by the Germain Funeral Home of Howard City, and a beautiful inlaid chancel chair. George Germain, now the Director of Facilities at MCC, remembers playing on the old organ when it was in his father's establishment (G. Germain communication). The following is a letter sent by George's father to Jean Brundage, Chairperson of Heritage Village when he donated the organ:

January 15, 2006
Dear Ms. Brundage:

The organ and seat I donated came from the old Buggert Farm north of Amble on Bailey Road. In the late 1970s, Adele Buggert Martin who lived alone in the farmhouse had a sale and I purchased it at the auction.

She told me that it originally belonged to her parents who I believe died before 1950. She remembered sitting around it and singing songs as it was played. A good guess for the age of the organ and seat would be that it was made in the 1890s and obviously it was taken good care of as it still works.

After I purchased it I placed it in the lounge at my former funeral home, The Germain Funeral Home, in Howard City. I remember it being played (by family request) at a couple of funerals probably for a much older person.

If I can offer anything further please let me know.
Sincerely,

David L. Germain

David L. Germain

The organ was made by the Chicago Cottage Organ Company, and has 61 keys, 12 stops, and 2 working pedals used to activate the bellows, which force the air through the reeds creating the sound. A piano was also discovered by Jesse Fox, and accompanies the organ on the church platform. Fox had asked Alex J. Kapteyn of Carson City to be on the lookout for a good piano that would withstand the ranging temperatures throughout the year in the Village Church. According to Kapteyn, there are only two or three brands that would work well. Shortly after the conversation, Kapteyn called from his shop and said, "I've got just the one." He transported it to the Village, and has maintained the piano ever since (Fox, telephone interview).

In the latter 1800s, the idea of having a piano in church was highly controversial among some parishioners, since the piano was identified with the saloon and bar room. Interestingly, many "Gospel Songs" in today's hymnbooks were bar-room tunes to which religious poetry was added. Some of those can be identified in the 50 hymnbooks donated to the Village Church by the First Congregational Church/United Church of Christ in Sheridan. The "Worshipping Church Hymnals" were dedicated in 1991 in memory of Steve Davis.

Even the inlaid chair on the platform has a story. It is a beautifully crafted hand-made chair, dark stained, having two grooves in each curved arm rest and all four curved legs with claw-like feet. The back rest exhibits an inlaid German design, crowned by a hand-carved relief. When Gary Hauck was giving a tour during the festival of 2009, Carl Schmidt, a gentleman from the community, entered the church and said, "I am the one who donated that chair. I bid on it at an auction because I thought it was a very attractive piece of furniture. But when I got it home, I felt a tad guilty, and decided to donate it to the Village." It is a beautiful addition to the church chancel.

Also on display in the Church is a beautiful Bible of the King James Version. Encased in glass, the gilded-cover Bible is a striking example of a family Bible that was often given to a new family on wedding day. An engraved gold plate on top of the case reads:

> **Given as a wedding gift from William Mook of Fenwick MI, to his wife Eva Sanborn, May 20, 1891. Bible donated by William's grandson & his wife, Carl & Ruth Allen, of Stanton MI.**

Embossed in gold on the left of the front cover of the Bible is the quotation "Thou shalt love the Lord thy God with all thy heart;" and on right, "Thou shalt love thy neighbor as thyself." In the middle are the words, "HOLY

BIBLE," with a clam shell on the middle upper left and four points, signifying creation and the four corners of the Earth. On the upper middle right, 12 square gem stones signify the 12 tribes of Israel and 12 disciples, and four points symbolize the four major prophets and four gospels. At the top of the front cover is a beautiful etching of the Lord's Supper, with the lamp of knowledge on the left, and the Eye of God on right, and at the bottom is the celestial city, or "New Jerusalem." Interestingly, since the King James Version of the Bible was translated in the year 1611, this year of 2011 marks the 400th anniversary of that important sacred text.

Mary Jane Bills, an instructor at Central Michigan University and former township clerk, has served as the Church docent. Since 2008, she has been joined by Gary Hauck, an ordained minister who also dons a parson's robe and stole for school tours and Festival. The Church is available for weddings at a rental fee of $250.00. On March 12, 2010, Hauck performed the wedding ceremony of his oldest son, Greg Hauck, to Rachel Czajkowski in the Village Church. Normally the Town Hall is used for the bride's preparation while the guests congregate in the church. On this occasion, however, the bride dressed in the Church as the guests roamed the village. She indicated that she would ring the steeple bell when she was ready, and everyone kept listening for that joyous sound. At last, the bell rang out and the happy guests entered to see the lovely bride in her full array. The ceremony then began. A brick in the sidewalk now reads, "Greg and Rachel Hauck – March 12, 2010."

The Heritage Village Church is now also used for the opening ceremony of the annual Festival, which is conducted at 11:00 on Thursday morning. Speakers for this event have included Rev. Bill Raymor, Rev. James Wilcox, and Rev. Gary Hauck. As Village Chair, Jean Brundage presents memorial gifts, and the Festival is officially opened with special music and prayer. Later during Festival, in addition to tours, the church hosts "The Story Lady" who entertains the children, and a Saturday afternoon hymn sing, led by pianist Bob Milne.

Upper photos: Ehle Barn and newly constructed Farm Equipment Shelter. Ehle Barn and Shoen Log House.

Lower : Barn interior and exterior during Festival.

17.

EHLE BARN

Originally located in Sheridan, this mortise and tenon barn was owned by Merle Ehle and was donated to the Village by Mr. Ehle's granddaughter, Tammy DuVall. Leonard Schrock of Vickeryville and his crew dismantled and reconstructed the barn at the Village in late 2006. Dale White was highly involved with this project, and maintains the barn. It now houses old farm equipment that is on display during the annual festival. White explains the barn was situated across from the Sheridan Hospital on Highway 66. In that location it had a basement under it that housed farm animals at one time. Dale shares, "The committee chose this project for me because I collect old gas engines and old farm tools. I willingly accepted because I enjoy woodworking and repairing things, and I also get to display some items of my collection and explain their uses to visitors during Festival" (D. White letter). In 2010, White joined Tom Learmont and Alvin Rush in building a large Farm Equipment Shelter near the Ehle Barn. The three-sided Farm Equipment Shelter is the most recent addition to Heritage Village, and will house many of the larger field implements that have been rusting while on display in the open air.

Photo collage: Members of the Benson and Gommesen Family present a Civil War re-enactment during Festival. Dave Gillette and Company entertain with dulcimers. Crafters Larry Pearson, Bill Ellsworth, and Larry Engle display and sell their handmade wares. Exhibits of the Montcalm Area Art Association, and tanners Eric Lau and Rand Miller.

18.

HERITAGE FESTIVAL AND SANTA'S SUPER SUNDAY

Heritage Festival

Of course, the highpoint of the year is the annual Heritage Festival conducted during the first Thursday through Saturday of August, when the Village comes to life with docents in period costume, Civil War reenactments, classes in the Gaffield School, an historical meeting at the Town Hall, a gospel hymn sing in the Village Church, and butter churning near the Sidney General Store.

The idea of a Festival began with the community and evolved over time. As noted earlier, the first celebration actually occurred in the fall of 1986 with the arrival of both the Gaffield School and Shoen Log House. For this reason, 2011 marks the 25th anniversary of the Village. But almost immediately, the idea of a summer celebration emerged. "Heritage Village began with a couple of buildings, no trees, and a desire to have a special summer event," Burns recalls. "The first few outings were hot, and with only a few volunteers and a handful of others attending. But this has grown over time and evolved into our annual Heritage Festival as it is today. As August approaches, everyone around now knows there's going to be food, a bake sale, music, flea market, and an opportunity to see history from the area" (Burns interview, 2011).

In 1987, the festival was billed as the "Montcalm Sesquicentennial Heritage Village Celebration" (Smith, Committee minutes). It ran a full week, from Monday, July 27 through Saturday, August 1st, 10 am to 4 pm and 7 pm to 9 pm Monday through Friday, and 10 am to 4 pm on Saturday. The list of special events included:

- School classes from the early 1900s in the Gaffield Schoolhouse
- Arts and crafts demonstrations in the Shoen Log House
- Flat River Antique Tractor and Machinery Club demonstrations
- Michigan Old Timers Band Concert
- First Lady Awards
- Spagetti dinner
- Square dance (in the MCC gym)
- A musical play of Michigan's history in the Barn Theater
- The Danish Folk High School Music Group
- Barbed-wire demonstration
- Medicine show
- Flat River Big Band Concert

Like Burns, others also remember the effort as quite ambitious for the small band of volunteers, with lots of planned events, but few who attended. The MCC Board of Trustees so appreciated this endeavor, that it issued the following resolution:

MONTCALM COMMUNITY COLLEGE
HERITAGE VILLAGE COMMITTEE
RESOLUTION

WHEREAS, the Montcalm Community College Board of Trustees is proud of our American, Michigan and Montcalm heritage, and

WHEREAS, the MCC Board of Trustees encourages and supports the study and preservation of local history, and

WHEREAS, the MCC Heritage Village Committee planned and implemented a sesquicentennial Heritage Village Celebration in the summer of 1987, and

WHEREAS, the MCC Heritage Village Committee has spent many hours organizing and preparing for the 1988 MCC Heritage Village Celebration so that others could enjoy, learn about, remember and appreciate our local history,

NOW, THEREFORE, BE IT RESOLVED, That the MCC Board

of Trustees expresses its appreciation to the MCC Heritage Village Committee for its commitment to the development of the Heritage Village project and celebration.

Beatrice Doser, Chairperson
Montcalm Community College
August 9, 1988

The 1988 Festival was simply called, the "Heritage Village Celebration," and ran for five days, Monday, August 8 through Friday, August 12. It featured many of the events from the previous year, along with horse and mule-drawn wagon rides, historical films and children's films in the Barn Theater, health clinics, milking demonstrations, baton twirlers, an antique car show, petting zoo, sing-along, and an old-fashioned picnic (Smith, Committee minutes). In coming years, the official name became, "The Heritage Festival," and the dates were set as the first Thursday through Saturday of August.

Even spelling bees were conducted during Festival, between the years of 1988 and 1992. In a memorandum dated August 6, 1992, Terry Smith wrote to Jean Brundage:

> Per your request, following is a brief critique of the Heritage Village Spelling Bee. On Thursday, July 30, MCC Dean of Liberal Arts and Business Dennis Mulder and I facilitated the 5th annual Heritage Village Spelling Bee. (I've served as judge and coordinator of the event since its inception in 1988. Les Morford hosted it and pronounced the words in 1988, 1989, 1990, and 1991. This year, he was unable to do so, and he asked Dean Mulder to take his place.)

> There were two divisions, as there have been each year. Division A was open to anyone up to those who have completed the seventh grade. Division B included all spellers who are entering the ninth grade in fall 1992 and are older.

> The spelling bee was publicized via a news release to local media (newspapers and radio stations).

> This year's bee ran about 1 hour in the Barn Theater. There were less than 10 people in the audience. First-place winners in each division were given a certificate for a Heritage Village T-shirt. Second-place

winners were given a certificate for a Heritage Village baseball cap. We sent each participant a certificate of achievement for participating. (Smith, Committee minutes)

Due to the decrease of numbers of participants and spectators, the spelling bee was discontinued. "But I guess that's the nature of evolving movements," Smith says today. "Interests change, and that's okay. We continue doing those activities that people enjoy" (Smith communication). The ongoing goal of the Heritage Village Committee is to make Festival a successful celebration of the area's past, while appealing to the interests and needs of today and the future.

Burns again shares:

Annually you see these people who come in the summer and participate in the Village—music makers, blacksmiths, and store-keepers. You also see younger people getting involved in the story-telling, selling their dill pickles and other homemade items. We now even have vintage baseball games along with the car show, quilt show, and other exhibits and displays that were added with time. Having been raised in the area, I connect with so many people during Festival that turn up here at the Village that wouldn't have come to the college otherwise. So it is a nice touching point for a reunion of sorts with the community college and is certainly a worthwhile endeavor.

One of the other things that strikes me as I meander through the Village during Festival is that many of these items are things that I myself have used! Some might be only 50-60 years old, and remind me that we are all a piece of history. These all bring back wonderful memories. I even enjoy seeing the horses as they pull the wagon around the Village at Festival. I love horses. As a youngster, we had workhorses. Each year, Fred Ehle comes out with his horses and uses them to pull the wagon. It's not a simple process. (Burns)

Burns' enthusiasm is reflected now by many in the community.

Recent Festivals have included "tanners" Eric Lau and Rand Miller and their displays of pelts normally situated just west of the Blacksmith Shop. Rand is a docent at the Michigan State Historical Museum, and travels to schools and organizations with his live demonstrations. Both Eric and Rand draw crowds of interested children and adults with their historical exhibitions during Festival (R. Miller telephone interview).

Civil War Reenactments are also featured each year with Tony Benson of McBride, his wife Cathy, and their boys, Clinton and Levi. They are joined by Mike and Deborah Gommesen of Howard City and their children, Faith, Hope, Charity, and Simon. With the military uniforms of the men and flowing period gowns of the ladies, they add much color and culture to the Festival experience. Visitors can examine their tents, cooking utensils, replicated weapons, and other authentic equipment. Since they camp in these tents during Festival, cook their own meals, churn their butter, and live just like those during the 1860s, the experience of watching and interacting with them is said to be like traveling back in time. Since the children are home-schooled, these events are part of their education and they have learned the historical information well. Even as they stroll through the other Village streets and buildings, they stay in character during the three days of Festival (T. Benson telephone interview). With this year's 150th anniversary of the Civil War, the 2011 Union encampment will be a highlight of the Heritage Festival.

Ragtime Piano of Bob Milne

For the past 14 years, the ragtime piano playing of Bob Milne has been associated with the celebration of the Heritage Festival. During that first, warm Friday evening in August, patrons fill the Barn Theater for a delightful evening of keyboard magic that transports the audience into the world of yesteryear. Mike Montgomery writes, "Bob is a wonderful musician and has a unique style because he didn't start out as a piano player. He started out as a French horn player, and then drifted into piano playing because pub owners were more willing to hire a solo pianist than a solo French hornist. It's basic economics. As a result, he taught himself some of the piano playing tricks. Effect, runs, and so on that make his act a really fun one to watch as well as to listen to" (qtd. in Milne iv).

Bob shares his own story of how he became involved at Heritage Village:

I was first supposed to come to Heritage Village in October of 1996. However, I suffered a serious broken leg one week before the concert and was hospitalized for a long time. The concert was canceled, of course. Then Jesse Fox contacted me about rescheduling for January, I believe it was. He had heard me somewhere north of Greenville, I don't remember where.

A wonderful lady named Valerie took care of the sound, lights and stage preparations. I later heard she had an amazing story of her own. After many years of living a rough life in Detroit, she fled until her car ran out of gas in front of Montcalm College. If I recall correctly, she decided this was an omen, so somehow enrolled and took every class you had to offer. Today she's very successful somewhere in your area.

There is a parallel here. I had actually quit playing the piano in 1990 after 25 years of playing in Detroit seafood houses, restaurants and bars. I, too, fled Detroit because of some dangerous situations that I won't even describe, but which helped me decide to find a different source of income. I banged around doing anything I could to earn a living for a few years, even resorting to my old profession as a pool player for a while. (Yes, playing pool for money was safer than playing the piano in those years.) But now a few churches called me up and asked if I'd play a program for them. I actually had to see if I still had a suit that fit to go to them. One of these churches was in your area, where I believe it was that Jesse heard me. When I finally arrived at your stage with a broken leg, I was in a wheelchair and barely able to function.

More people started calling me back in those years. I didn't realize that what I did was suitable for concert halls, so had never looked in that direction. Your little concert hall was one of the first I ever played in. Things began to change after that. A few years later I played in east coast amphitheatres with 5000 people present. Soon I was playing over 200 performances a year.

Like Valerie, Montcalm College and the Heritage Village acted as a "Phoenix bird" catalyst for me. I have been very pleased and honored that you've invited me back every year. It's very special to me. No one ever forgets a helping hand.

Oh, yes. The wheelchair is long gone. Except every time I come back to Heritage Village, I still look at the steps to the stage that Jesse somehow hauled me up. I can still feel the pangs in my leg from the third step for some reason. (Milne e-mail)

Through a prior arrangement by Jesse Fox, the Alex J. Kapteyn Piano Company, Inc. of Carson City provides (free of charge) a quality piano each year for the Festival Ragtime Concert. Alex personally delivers the piano, and George Germain (MCC Director of Facilities) and his crew use a forklift to hoist the piano onto the stage of the old Barn Theater.

During the 2009 Festival, Bob meandered over to the Village Church on Saturday afternoon and began playing hymns on the piano. Before long, the church was filled with young and old alike. It turned into a spontaneous hymn sing, and the strains filled Main Street. As a result, a "Bob Milne Hymn Sing" was added to the scheduled events for 2010 (with another full house), and will continue as yet another annual feature.

Santa's Super Sunday

Every year, the Village is open during the first Sunday of December for Santa's Super Sunday, when hundreds of children and their parents enjoy a stroll or hay wagon ride around the magical setting. Brundage recalls:

When we first began participating in Santa's Super Sunday, Harriet Olsen made chicken noodle soup for those of us who were going to work as volunteers during that very cold day, being the first Sunday in December. She would bring a big cooler with the soup, silverware, cups and coffee, and we would eat in the cold, sitting there in the Shoen Log House. One time we spilled some hot chocolate on the floor and it froze immediately! Another time, one of the visiting children spilled his hot chocolate in my purse. At first, we met at the Log House then later, we met in the Town Hall. It was hard for Harriet to leave the Log House for those outings, since she and her husband, Clarence, had a cabin in Stanton and had a barn filled with old tools. Ironically, Harriet always dressed up with a beautiful dress and high heel shoes. Harriet and Clarence later hosted the Town Hall. When we went to visit Sauder Village in Ohio, we got the idea of a furnace or a pot belly stove. As a result, we soon put one in the Town Hall, Log House, and School (but that one has a big crack in it and it needs to be fixed.) We need to heat every building. At first, I started volunteering for the December event with crafts on campus. Now that I worked the Village in that cold weather, I realized how important it was for us to get those stoves! (Brundage interview).

Gary L. Hauck

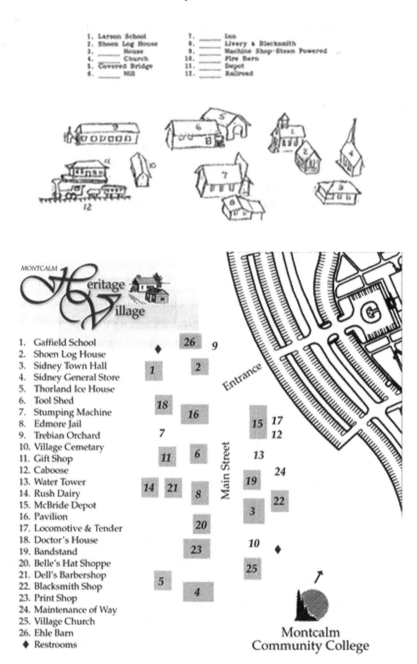

Diagram at top of page: Jesse Fox's original sketch (final draft) of
how Heritage Village could someday appear, as presented to the
MCC Board of Trustees on October 3, 1986 (courtesy of Jesse Fox).
Bottom: A map of Heritage Village today (courtesy of Jody Hedrick).

102

19.

THE PRESENT AND FUTURE OF HERITAGE VILLAGE

In an effort to explore other possibilities for the Village, some members traveled to White Pine Village in Ludington, as well as the Historic Sauder Village in Archbold, Ohio, and returned with many creative ideas. Refinements are going on all the time. For an example, the street signs were donated and installed around 2005. Today, school and organizational tours are given by appointment, and of course, the Village comes alive during each annual festival and Santa's Super Sunday.

"There are more pieces that can come together," says Burns. "There is still more potential. Perhaps in time we'll see a little tighter tie between the histories taught at the college and Heritage Village." He continues:

> And as the history of the college becomes more developed, perhaps we'll see the broader context of these mutual histories and have a better grasp of it. But I do not wish to see the college take over the Village. When VIPs come in and take over a project like this, the community element soon becomes lost, and the spirit of volunteerism vanishes. Of course, some things may run their course, and that is only natural. I was opposed to taking it over as a college, because when this committee meets and works, it is they who bring the history with them! The community, it is theirs! This is ideal. This is the preferred state and vision of Heritage Village. If the school took it over, it wouldn't be the same. (Burns)

Certainly, this is the view shared by both the college and the members of the village committee. But as the faithful core of volunteers continues to advance in years, the desire is for younger and newer blood to catch the vision and carry on the work.

Another need is the ongoing evaluation and careful selection of acquired artifacts. According to Burns, "We've had folks who want to just get rid of stuff. So it is a task to sort through it all so that it is value added. Over the years we've had people call and say, 'This should be in Heritage Village. Can you come over and pick it up?' And my response normally has been, 'Well, let's see and talk about it.' When it is a good match, it makes for such a good connection with people of the community" (Burns).

The vision of Burns, Brundage, and the members of the committee is for the Heritage Village to be a place for the teaching of the history of the country, state, and local region, cultivating an appreciation for it contextually and programmatically. They also want the Village to be a special place for weddings, services, music, and much celebration. "It is an opportunity for more culture and cultural awareness in the heart of Montcalm County" (Burns).

Possible thoughts for the future have included a stronger tie with the Barn Theater, Farmhouse, Kenneth Lehman Trails, and the Frederick Meijer Trail (having a connecting loop to the Meijer Trail that surrounds the village), the addition of a Native American encampment, and a Heritage Village Saloon. More development is certainly inevitable. Others speak of making it a destination throughout the year, with easier access, parking, an information center, adjoining park, and kiosks. With the current sewer line, there is already a right of way that crisscrosses the county. It would not take much to intersect the Meijer Trail. However, with the all-volunteer model, no one is projecting that the village should be open throughout the year, given the limited amount of time and energy that people could provide. If nothing else, fall seems to be an inviting and magical time of the year, when many believe the Village could serve as a wonderful place to visit. Jean Brundage reflects:

> Some people say we have enough now, but I say we need to keep adding buildings, new ideas, and well-selected artifacts. People will not come back if we don't have change. Others say we don't have enough people. We actually still have about 20-30 faithful members today, including people like Fred Ehle, Phil Frisbie, Dale White, and Tom Learmont. These individuals have done a lot of the manpower things. Not everyone is able to use a hammer. Many others volunteer

as well, and when a need is communicated, we always seem to have the bases covered. (Brundage interview)

Interestingly, Heritage Village is also continuing to develop new relationships in the county. In 2010, Bob Clingenpeel, Director of Montcalm County's Commission on Aging, partnered with Heritage Village for the Commission's "1st Annual Harvest Picnic." The picnic on Thursday, September 16 at Heritage Village included a car show, health care vendors, candidate meet-and-greet, pig roast, chili cook-off, magic show, quilt show, DJ music, and Village tours. A total of eighteen senior groups from around the county participated, including MCC's Life-Long Learners who took the opportunity to promote non-traditional student classes available at the Montcalm Community College. During the 2011 anniversary season, this function will become incorporated into the Annual Heritage Festival on August 4-6, and future Annual Festivals. The members of the Village are thankful for this new partnership, and the additional energy and enthusiasm that Mr. Clingenpeel brings to the planning and preparation for this event.

What is the vision for the future? One thing is sure – the Village will remain a vital part of MCC's heritage, and that of the entire county.

Photo Above: Top row – Gary Hauck, Alvin Rush,
Dale White, Sharon Ritter, Larry Beard.

Bottom row—Vivian Hey, Margaret Rush, Marge Stone-Waldron, Chairperson
Jean Brundage, Judy White, Kathy Beard, and Miriam Zimmerman meet
for the April 2011 Committee meeting. (Not all members included.)

Lower Photo: Miriam Zimmerman, Kathy Beard, Chairperson
Jean Brundage, Lou Kitchenmaster (standing), Dale White,
Judy White, and Larry Beard deliberate during the March
2011 Committee meeting. (Not all members included.)

20.

MEET SOME OF THE COMMITTEE MEMBERS & VOLUNTEERS

The following Heritage Village Committee members and volunteers responded to a questionnaire and sent letters to the author. Please note that this is a representative group of the many individuals who have helped to make Heritage Village what it is today. Sincere apologies are given to those whose information is not included. Appreciation is extended to every member, volunteer, and contributor.

Kathy Beard enjoyed coming to the annual Festival, became "hooked," and joined Heritage Village in 2006 (K. Beard). In addition to now being responsible for the Shoen Log House, Kathy assists with both the Spring and Fall fund-raising dinners, works the Festival, and explains life in the 1860s to visiting school groups during the spring tour season. "I became a member of the Heritage Village as I wanted to see it be preserved for generations to come. I really enjoy it" (K. Beard). Kathy retired in 2001 from Huntington National Bank, and enjoys crocheting and reading mystery books. She and her husband, Larry, have lived in the Six Lakes area for over 40 years. Kathy states, "I feel we are very fortunate to have a historic village so close. I think everyone should come and see it. I would like to see more people get involved in Heritage Village, especially younger people so that it can continue for years to come."

Larry Beard, like his wife Kathy, joined the Village in 2006. He has always loved history, and has had an interest in how people lived in the 1800s and early twentieth century. Larry is the volunteer in charge of the McBride's

Heritage Village Committee Members:

Al and Margaret Rush

Bill Raymor

Carol Lau

Cheryl Smith

Dale and Judy White

Earl Buskirk

Eugene Rydahl

Fred Ehle*

Gary Hauck

Ilene Thompson*

Jean Brundage*

Jesse and Marilyn
Fox*

Kathern Hansen

Larry and Kathleen
Beard

Lou Kitchenmaster Marge Stone-
Waldron

Max and Flora
Phelps*

Miriam Zimmerman

Pat and Al Buchholtz

Randy and Elle Kempf

Ron Springsteen

Rosemary Long*

Ruth Hansen*

Shannon Kilduff

Sharon McInnis

Tom and Ruth
Learmont*

Vivien Hey

Life-time members*

Depot, but admits, "I did not choose the building, but was asked to help out because the gentleman in charge at that time, Keith McInnis, was having some health concerns. However, if I were to have picked a building it would have been either the Depot or the Store." He continues to explain, "The reason I would have picked the store was because when I was four years old, I played in the upstairs of the Sidney General Store. Secondly, I would have picked the Depot since my grandfather worked on the C & O Railroad in Ohio, and because I have always been interested in trains" (L. Beard). Larry writes:

> Every year since we have been members we have helped set up and worked at both of the spring and fall dinners, and are always there to have our buildings open for touring groups, visitors, and for Festival. During Festival time, I have had people come in who had actually been in the building when it was a working depot at McBride's. They have told me things about the layout of the building's interior as it was then. I've also had the opportunity to explain the building through an interpreter for individuals from France, and for some children who were hearing impaired. (L. Beard)

Larry is retired from Tower Automotive in Greenville, and likes to golf, fish, hunt, do crossword puzzles, and travel throughout the United States. He is a life-long resident of Montcalm County, and spent two years in Sidney.

Ruth Bedore was among those who explored the possibility of establishing an historical village in Montcalm as early as 1985. She was interested in re-creating life in the time period of her parents and grandparents who lived on a farm in Connecticut. Although she was not assigned to any building in particular, Ruth was involved during the summer Festivals for over 10 years. She remembers when the Festival quilt show used to be in the MCC Farmhouse, and recalls one year in particular when she won a beautiful quilt of satin in a fundraising raffle.

Ms. Bedore is a graduate of Boston University, and came to Michigan to begin her practice as a physical therapist. This is where she met her husband, Cliff, and the two were married the same day he graduated from Northern Michigan College. Cliff Bedore served as the second president of Montcalm Community College. The Bedores have lived in Greenville for 47 years, and will celebrate their 70th wedding anniversary in June of 2011. Writing of the importance of Heritage Village she states, "I want my descendents to be aware of changes in the county. We need to know what our ancestors faced and where we might like to go. Heritage Village gives us a good starting point" (Bedore).

Jean Brundage is a charter member of the Heritage Village Association and has served as the Chairperson for the past 22 years, having first served as Secretary and then Vice President. As a member of the Board of Trustees at Montcalm Community College, Jean was asked by then board Chairperson, Bea Doser, to attend the Heritage Village Association meetings as a representative of the college. Although she is responsible for the entire Village, Jean's building assignment has been the Sidney General Store from the time it was moved to the Village. She recalls, "It needed someone to take care of it, and I was chosen by the committee to do so. It was only a shell when it arrived. It had nothing in it. Over the years, items have been donated or purchased to make it what it is today" (J. Brundage letter). She continues, "The store is a favorite of visitors, as it reminds them of their past. Also, when we have children on tour we give them a piece of candy and tell them it once sold for one cent." She laughingly reports that her husband, Bob (who drove a people mover during Festival), tried to talk her out of her involvement with the Village because she spent too much time there. She does confess:

> I've been a volunteer since the Village was formed, and have helped wherever needed. I have conducted tours, helped with dinners, painted buildings, worked in the Depot to clean it up, and several other projects. To me, being a member of Heritage Village has been a great experience. I have very nice memories of the children who have visited over the years. It is also fun to think of new things we can add each year to make it bigger and better so that everyone can enjoy it. For some reason, I have always enjoyed "old things." I quilt, have made baskets, and took nine years of painting from Nancy Fox at MCC. Although I am now retired, I still enjoy my involvements with the Village, and continue to serve on the college's Board of Trustees for more than 26 years. (Brundage letter)

Robert Buskirk entered the volunteer ranks of Heritage Village 18 years ago after retiring from Hitachi. He became interested in the growing project and wanted to help with his carpentry and painting skills. Although Belle's Hat Shop was his major project, he has engaged in the repairing and painting of most of the buildings in the Village and the procuring of the pews for the

Church. He still works his farm and enjoys whittling and wood-working, but his delight is "helping to preserve our heritage" (Buskirk letter).

Geraldine Christensen began her relationship with Heritage Village in 1986, when she was recruited by her sister, Hazel Smith, the first Chairperson. She says, "When she became enthused and asked for your help, it was hard to tell her no" (Christensen). Geraldine spent most of her volunteer time at the Gaffield School, since she was a retired teacher, had attended a one-room school as a student, and taught in a one-room school as a teacher. She is most fascinated by the pictures on the back wall of old schools and their students, samples of old textbooks used years ago, and the special flooring of the school house. Geraldine wrote the curriculum for grades K-3 for the first year's demonstration, and acted as the building's host on many occasions. Mr. Christensen, Geraldine's husband, and also a one-room school teacher, supervised and taught the games played by the school children during the recesses of 1986. Among her special memories are the parades that Dorothea Ellsworth arranged for the Village, the historical dramas that Jeanette Emmons supervised, the town hall meetings, and all the action at the school house.

Geraldine attended Pleasant Hill Rural School, Lakeview High, County Normal (1939-40), and later took college classes at Central Michigan University, Michigan State University, Western Michigan University, Eastern Michigan University, and Montcalm Community College (art classes). She received her B.S. degree in 1968 and taught for 27 years, raised five children, has ten grandchildren, and nine great-grandchildren. "I guess my main interest is in children," she writes. "<u>I</u> like <u>kids</u>" (Christensen).

Lillian Christophersen was invited by Hazel Smith to join Heritage Village during the early years, and appointed her to serve on the committee to move the Sidney Town Hall. Hazel recalls, "I thought it was a wonderful idea as I like old things and think they should be saved for future people to see how the past worked" (L. Christophersen letter). Lillian retired in 1999 as the head cook of Central Montcalm Middle School. She has lived here all her life, and attended the Sidney School from 1st – 6th grades. Circumstances have prevented her involvement at the Village in recent years, and she misses those days of participation. She shares this information:

> My mother, Alma Corfixsen, was a teacher at the Sidney School in
> the 30s. She was instrumental in getting the merry-go-round as the
> students had nothing to play on. The swings were put there when I

attended in the 40s and early 50s. When the Township Board was going to take it out of the park, I asked if I could have it, but when they said it would go to the Village, I was happy! It had a warped board on it when I was a kid, and so we called it the "slippery board," because we could slide off it.

I have donated boxes of old school books that had been my mother's, along with her class picture from County Normal and her old valentines from the 1930s, in addition to a bedspread and curtains for the Doctor's House. (Christophersen)

Jesse Fox has been a part of Heritage Village from the beginning, 25 years ago. MCC President Don Burns asked Jesse to make arrangements to accept and move the Shoen Log House to the campus from nearby Crystal in 1986. And in October of that year, before the MCC Board of Trustees would grant final approval for the idea of a complete Village, Jesse was asked to prepare an initial planning map of how the Village might someday look. Since then, Fox has also been heavily involved with the Doctor's House, Village Church, and Thorland Ice House. The committee asked Jesse and his wife to finish the Doctor's House (roof, siding, flooring, painting, and wallpapering), replace the school windows, organize a painting party for the exterior of the Village Church, varnish the interior of the church (along with his wife, Marilyn), and install the brick sidewalk in front of the church.

It was Fox who located a suitable piano for the church, did the electrical work in the Rush Dairy, and moved the heavy soda fountain from the Depot to the Dairy. After hearing Bob Milne play his ragtime piano at an area church, Jesse arranged for Milne to play annual concerts during Festival to benefit the treasury. Among many other projects, Jesse has served as a docent during children's tours in the Depot, Steam Engine, and Town Hall as needed; drove people mover (golf cart) during festival; collected many items for the yard sales and stored them in the Icehouse; helped to clean, organize, furnish, and staff the Rush Dairy; cleaned and caulked many of the buildings throughout the Village; and had a role in the moving of the Steam Engine.

Fox reflects, "I enjoy making history come alive for younger folks. And, I enjoy hearing old-timers explain how they used an item on their farm or whatever, when they were young. Story telling is such an important part of what we do." He continues, "I have clear memories of the Festivals down through the years, and the moving of the locomotive, but what I am most thankful for is the dedication and hard work of the members of our committee who are mostly retired or up in years." (J. Fox letter)

Fox arrived at Montcalm Community College from Illinois in 1973 to teach in the Aviation Maintenance-Technology Program. In 1983, that program was discontinued, all the equipment was sold, and he was appointed as the Dean of Occupational Education. Although Jesse retired in 1989, he has continued to maintain a high level of involvement. He shares:

> I enjoy helping young people understand the building of this country. I'm interested in all forms of transportation and mechanization. After being an active member for these 25 years, I have decided to go inactive. I'm proud to have been a part of the building years of the Village, but the physical work of maintaining the buildings and working the projects has now become a challenge for me. I wish the Village ongoing success in the years to come." (J. Fox letter)

Marilyn Fox became involved with Heritage Village around 1997, when she began to know Jesse Fox, now her husband. She was impressed with "the good people of the committee, and their desire to help preserve examples of our heritage" (M. Fox). Marilyn became an active participant with projects at the Rush Dairy, Village Church, and the Doctor's House. "We desired to make the Dairy into an ice cream shop, complete with soda fountain. We also had doctor's equipment and house furnishings that needed a good place for display. I was on the church planning committee, and wanted to see it through to completion" (M. Fox). She continues, "Jesse and I found donors of the ice cream tables and chairs, and operating equipment for the Doctor's House. I made the church runner from a piece of cast-off carpeting, which I halved and joined end-to-end, and helped Jesse with the Bob Milne Concerts, providing cookies and ice tea to all who attended."

Marilyn started the yard sale to raise money and ran that event for several years. She also served as a docent in the Dairy on many occasions, helped Jesse install the brick sidewalk in front of the Village Church, varnished much of the church interior, and helped complete the interior of the Doctor's House. For Marilyn, the most memorable aspects of her time at the Village include the arrival of the locomotive, seeing the completion of the Village Church, seeing the dedication of the members, and observing the leadership and determination of Jean Brundage as the Chairperson. Mrs. Fox has always lived in the area and still has family here. She worked at Frigidaire while her husband worked at the college. Marilyn loves the Village and exclaims, "I wish we could get everybody in the county to visit and learn about our Village" (M. Fox).

Maxine Harris was one of the four who traveled to Ludington 25 years ago to explore the Historic White Pine Village, and returned to Montcalm with the idea of replicating that concept on the campus of Montcalm Community College. She served as one of the first volunteers assigned by Hazel Smith to the Shoen Log House, and remembers the first groups of children who visited. Maxine also planned and arranged twelve summer bus trips to various locations in Michigan during a three-year period to help raise money for the growing Village. One special memory is of a two bus-load trip to Tulip Time in Holland, Michigan. Maxine loves Heritage Village because it gives a "peek at the past" (Harris). Harris is a retired elementary teacher who "likes kids and adults, and enjoys gardening and travel."

Vivian Hey has been a farmer's wife, hospital secretary, and administrative assistant for the Secretary of State's office. She has served on the Sidney Township Board for 40 years, and is still active as the Deputy Treasurer. Hey joined the Heritage Village Committee in 2003 when Harriet Olson asked her to assist in the Sidney Town Hall. Each spring, she explains the "old-time" use of the town hall building to school children's tour groups. During Festival, Vivian also manages the Gift Shop and the Welcome Booth at the Village entrance. Vivian states, "I so enjoy seeing the interest of students, and the 'I remember that' expression of older visitors. I'm pleased that this is something I can still do at age 88, and hear all the children's responses when we explain the 'Good Ole Days'" (Hey).

Tom Learmont became involved in 1995 and has continued to be an active member since then, thus a total of about 15 years. He writes:

> Although I have played a leading part in the development and maintenance of the Village, I have never been one of the officers. I have always been interested in the preservation of old buildings and the viewing of old ghost towns, especially old mining towns out West. I retired in 1993 and moved from the Detroit area to Gowen, where we spent about one year setting up our new home, after which I was not sure what I was going to do with my time. One day while out looking at the College, I observed the old buildings in the Village

across College Drive. At that time, the General Store was looking in poor shape as the paint was peeling badly and I thought, "Gosh! That could use some help!" So, I began asking around about the buildings and learned of the Association, what it was trying to do, that I could join the group and assist with the maintenance. Thus began my membership in the group.

Oddly enough, there is no one particular building for which I am most responsible. For about three years after the caboose arrived I was assigned to that, but then it was transferred to others. My involvement in the Village began slowly and as time moved on and the group gained greater confidence in my abilities, I took on a greater role in the operation, building and maintenance of the village. When I began, the leaders were Jean Brundage, Fred Ehle, Harriet Olsen, Rosemary Long, Phil Frisbee and Edna Hansen. Fred was the leader in building and maintaining the buildings, thus I assisted him on different projects. I have done much as a volunteer over the years. I will approach this in a somewhat systematic way not by date or events. For a few years, I spent time in the spring assisting with the tours of school children, and during the summer Festival conducting tours of the Caboose, Steam Engine and Depot Complex as well as in the Jail. I also assisted on a limited basis with some of the Association dinners. My major contribution has been in the development and maintenance of the buildings, but I also organized and assisted in different repair and painting projects, including the General Store, Town Hall, Jail, Depot, Doctor's House, and other buildings. I suggested we needed some information at each building, so that as people walked around, they would learn something about what they were looking at. The idea took hold, so Edna Hansen and I developed the information to be presented on the different placards, which are now located throughout the Village. I contacted a sign manufacturer who made the placards that I attached to the wooden posts I made.

I have many memories of things associated with the Village, most of them great. I will mention a few. My most enjoyable memory is working with Don Hansen as we spent so much time together in the repair and painting of the Depot. Don was a great person and a true pleasure to be associated with. A now-funny memory is when I had all of the placards constructed and ready to install; Edna and I went out and placed stakes in the ground where we wanted to locate them. The next day when I went out to begin installing them, I found all of the stakes were pulled! Ivan was there and said we could not put in the post as he needed to mow and they would be in his way. I was upset at the time, so I went to Jean and said, "You need to decide if you want them, and if so, you need to tell Ivan to leave them alone!" As you can see, they are now neatly in place. I greatly enjoyed the time I spent working with many of the great Association members.

As I stated earlier I love to see old buildings and items of historical value preserved for those of the next generation, so they can better understand what has transpired in the past. The best example is the joy of seeing the expression on the faces of young children as they tour the different buildings and especially the Caboose.

I was born and raised in a small town in Michigan's copper mining district, and greatly enjoyed my life there as I had all the freedom to do and go wherever I wanted. I spent many days tramping through the forest, fishing with our little boat, and helping my dad on different carpentry jobs he did. Following high school I attended as a commuter, Michigan College of Mining and Technology, where I received my BS degree in Mechanical Engineering. I then spent the next 35 years in lower Michigan, working for different elements of the U.S. Defense Department in quality control. For the last 15 years of that time I was on the staff of the Program Manager for the M60 and later the M-1 Abrams Tanks. After retirement we moved to Gowen as we both enjoyed being in the country and much preferred the western side of the state to that of the eastern side. I had no connection with either the community or the College. I enjoyed fishing, hiking and camping along with most other outdoor sports. I greatly enjoyed traveling in the western states, viewing old mining towns, hiking in the mountains and canoeing rivers. I also enjoy doing some carpentry work, and being at Heritage Village provides me that opportunity. I am also a member of the Keweenaw Historical Society and, at times, have done work with that group. (Learmont letter)

Valgeen Mack (deceased) is remembered by his wife as having had an active role in Heritage Village over the years. She writes, "Val passed away two years ago. He would be very happy to be included in this written document" (K. Mack). "He liked to help people, and thought that showing life in the olden times was good for the young people." Val was instrumental in getting the McBride's Depot moved to the Village, and did much work on the inside of the Caboose as well. Mr. Mack was active in the Vestaburg Lions' Club, and served as its president in 2003-2004. He worked for the Department of Natural Resources, and has always had a strong interest in the development of Montcalm Community College, where several of his family attended. He believed that the historical Village was good for both the College and the community.

Mildred Mahan was one of the founders of the Heritage Village. Twenty-five years ago, she took Maxine Harris, Rosemary Long, and Hazel Smith to visit a restored historical village in Ludington. "Historic White Pine Village opened in 1976 and is an historic village of over 29 museum buildings and sites of history dedicated to preserving and presenting Mason County's past. The buildings contain thousands of signs, artifacts and archives that help interpret their place in history" (www.historicwhitepinevillage.org/). After seeing this village, the four women thought they might be able to copy their idea in Montcalm, and that it might be an interesting addition to the Community College. Hazel Smith had just retired from teaching, and decided to move forward with that idea. Mildred shares, "We planted the idea, and it developed beautifully!" (Mahan). Hazel is now deceased, but Mildred, Maxine, and Rosemary continue to enjoy what the Village has become today. "I saw the Heritage Village grow with many volunteer helpers. It truly has become a positive aspect of Montcalm Community College."

Mildred was present for the arrival of the Gaffield School and the Shoen Log House, and witnessed the ceremony when the Shoen Family made their presentation to MCC. "The Shoen family shared many interesting stories and facts that particularly caught my interest" (Mahan). For this reason, Mahan volunteered to be as assistant with the Log House, and worked with Maxine Harris and others presenting information about the cabin to the Village's first visitors. Mildred worked in the county for 21 years, and served as a home economist for the Michigan State University Extension.

Bob Marston was a member of the Board of Trustees for Montcalm

Community College when Heritage Village began, and continues in that capacity today. At that time, he also chaired the area's Sesquicentennial Committee and worked for the Montcalm Area Intermediate School District. For these reasons, he became instrumental in the acquisition, move, and site preparation of the Gaffield School, the first building to become a part of what is today, Heritage Village. Although Marston is not currently a member, his former company of Marston Enterprises is a life member (Marston).

Clarence and Harriet Olson (deceased) always had a love for the history of this region. Together, they served in the Central Montcalm Historical Society and the North Sidney Church and Cemetery Historical Society. After joining Heritage Village in the early years, they adopted the Sidney Town Hall as their project, and poured many days and hours into it. As a World War II veteran and farmer, Clarence had a passion for explaining relics of the past. As secretary of the Montcalm Soil Conservation District, Harriet enjoyed writing, and so became the author of the early township plays presented in the Town Hall. "They have tried to preserve artifacts from the area and hope[d] their labors will help present and future generations maintain a link with their ancestral heritage" (Olson, *North Sidney* 180-182). In one of her own poems she wrote:

Storms will come and the winds may blow,

Trees that are weakened will be harvested so.

We, too, shall fall one by one

When our mission here on the good earth is done. (p. 182)

A picture tribute to both Harriet and Clarence Olson hangs on the south wall inside the Town Hall today. The caption below the photo reads, "Clarence and Harriet Olson: THANK YOU for your dedication in helping to preserve Montcalm County 'Memories.'"

Flora Phelps began her volunteer work in 1996, when she worked at Heritage Village as a Master Gardener with Elaine Johnson, helping wherever needed and doing whatever was necessary, such as cleaning up around the Village and painting railings in readiness for the annual Festival. In 1997 she assisted with the log cabin, and today is responsible for the Doctor's House. She explains:

I was asked to do the Doctor's House by the Heritage Village group. It is one that is featured when schools come for end of the year field trips to help educate youth from most of Montcalm County and surrounding areas on the way things were in the "early days." I am the primary host for this building at those times and at Festival time, when it and the other buildings are open to the public to acquaint them with the way things were in days gone by.

For many years Max and I did mission work. I am a Master Gardener and help raise plants in my flower garden for their annual plant sale, volunteer at the Baby Pantry, have been involved with 4-H, help with local church functions and host church groups, belong to the Gideons and the Entrican Arbor of Gleaner's, and help others wherever needed. (F. Phelps)

Flora notes that her two most memorable occasions of Heritage Village were the dedication of the Village Church, and the day of the gazebo [Bandstand] dedication.

I am a member of Heritage Village because I like antiques. I enjoy being a part of it and teaching and sharing about the past with others during the Heritage Festival and at the other times when we open the buildings to let others see what life was like in earlier times. My hobbies are reading, gardening, working in missions with my husband and volunteering over the years. My husband encouraged me to take the Master Gardener course. I have attended short courses at MCC and am certified in floral design from MSU. Thus, I've been able to share my love of gardening with others through speaking engagements, as well. I really hope that Heritage Village will always be a part of the community and remain an active and viable asset to the area. (F. Phelps)

Max Phelps first became involved in 1995-96, when he helped his wife, Flora, and Mary and Carlton Ferguson put in antique roses from Grand Rapids and prepared them for winter by bedding them in. He's been a part of Heritage Village ever since that time. He writes:

In 1997 my wife, Flora, was asked to help with the log cabin and I helped with my carpentry skills by fixing up anything that needed it. Then, of course, in 2000 I remodeled and restored the Doctor's House.

I have helped many young people with remodeling to help them get started, worked with 4-H, I've done mission work for many years, working mostly as a carpenter, and I helped with handicap construction at Spring Hill Camp.

My most memorable memories are of the Doctor's House in particular. I am a member of Heritage Village because I think it's important to keep history alive. I like to hunt and fish and do carpentry. I took a course to learn building fireplaces and I've taught others masonry skills. I've built a total of 17 fieldstone fireplaces, including a large one in our home. I hope that people will continue to be interested in Heritage Village. (M. Phelps)

Sharon Ritter began her role as the "teacher" of Gaffield School 11 years ago, taking over from Eleanor Lantz. She describes her responsibilities as "mostly speaking to area school students who visit during the spring about how a one-room school functioned, and teaching during the three-day annual Festival. I also have served as Treasurer for the past four years, helped paint and clean before Festival, and helped set up for the yard sale" (Ritter). She continues, "We have a small, active committee, and I sincerely want the Village to continue. I'm happy for my role, since it helps me keep my 'finger in the pie' of education. I believe I am still helping to educate both students and adults. Many people have never visited the Village and are missing such a great opportunity and wonderful experience" (Ritter).

Alvin Rush is the owner of A & E Sawmill, and was the sawyer for quite a bit of the lumber to construct some of the buildings which were erected on site at Heritage Village. This is what began his involvement with the Village, sparked by his desire to preserve part of the region's past. Rush shares, "I enjoy my volunteer work with the Heritage Village group. I am a member of the Entrican Arbor of Gleaner's where we do Samaritan projects throughout the year in the surrounding area. I also serve on the boards of the Michigan Association of Timbermen and the Montcalm County Farm Bureau and their state Forestry Advisory Committee and on my township's Planning Commission." He continues:

> I am a member of Heritage Village because I think it is important to keep heritage and history alive. I was born and raised on a dairy farm, grew up with dairy. I worked in a factory until I had the opportunity to work with my brother in the woods, processing timber. Soon I had to choose, and the love of the forest and woods became my lifetime

vocation. I've been owner of Rush's Forest Products for well over 40 years and have one son who has worked in the business since age 14. He has now taken over the business.

Work was my hobby for many years because of my love of the woods and forestry. Now I like to travel, when possible, particularly with our fifth wheel camper and enjoy seeing new territories.

We need new volunteers and more young people to be able to keep Heritage Village going. Valuable history of the area in which we all grew up is within the boundaries of the Village and is a hands-on history lesson right here in our own backyard. My desire is that it never dies. (A. Rush)

Margaret Rush is in her fourth year of involvement at Heritage Village. Her aunt, Marion Hunsicker, was a retired school teacher and highly active with the Village. Margaret reports that her aunt, "always talked about the importance of keeping history alive for others or it would some day be lost. She did chair caning and mostly rug hooking demonstrations (not latch hook) during the Heritage Festival" (M. Rush). Margaret continued to explain that even when Marion could no longer drive due to macular degeneration of her eyes, she was able to participate thanks to Clarence and Harriet Olson, who provided transportation for her. But, there were other influences on Margaret as well:

My mother and stepfather, Ana and Hans Larsen, were very active with the Village. Hans was the Fairplains Township Treasurer for many years, and was instrumental in providing historical information about the Amsden area near Fenwick where they lived. So, I've wanted to continue what was important to them; that's part of my own heritage, as I look at it. And then, I want to support my husband with his continued interest in keeping the Rush Dairy legacy alive.

I'm probably mostly responsible in helping Flora Phelps with the Doctor's House; secondly, Rush Dairy. After I started coming to the Heritage Village meetings and plans were getting underway for the Festival, I learned that I would be helping Mrs. Phelps. That was wonderful for me because she's known me since I was very little, and, in fact, did our wedding flowers from her garden when Al and I were married. Secondly, of course, is helping Al with the Rush Dairy building and the salvaged components of his family's milk bottling equipment which he grew up with.

I was a 4-H leader for about 25 years and 4-H is still dear to my heart. Now, I'm involved with the Entrican Arbor or Gleaner's where we do many Samaritan projects around the area each year along with Heritage Village; and I support my husband with the organizations that he belongs to.

I'm a member of the Heritage Village group because of my interest in antiques, the likes of which I grew up with, and in wanting to keep those real stories alive for those today who have no idea what it was like to live in the 'old days'.

I was born and raised in this same community, married and raised a family in this area. I've worked as a teacher aide (as they were called then) so I know many whom I knew when they were small; I still keep my LPN license. I've worked a short time in real estate and worked for a world-wide company in their customer service department. My most loved hobbies are music and horses, which I've enjoyed since I was very small and gardening. I love to travel and learn about new places in this beautiful U.S.A. and hope to go to Alaska again. (M. Rush)

Eugene Rydahl joined Heritage Village in 2002 at the invitation of Harriet Olson, because of his interest in history. Dr. Rydahl holds a Ph.D. in Theatre History (East Saginaw, Mighigan), and taught in that field for 36 years at the University of Iowa, Eastern Illinois University, and Central Michigan University. Bringing this background to the committee, he was asked to take over the writing and directing of the Sidney Township Hall dramatic plays of the "early days," author the township histories, and produce CDs of these histories. Dr. Rydahl says of his experiences at Heritage Village, "I love being a volunteer! It's fun" (Rydahl).

William Seiter joined in the earliest discussions to acquire buildings and form the Village during the 1980s. He was a member of MARSP, a formal organization of retired teachers interested in obtaining a one-room school to be maintained as an example of early rural education in Michigan. Dr. Seiter is a retired teacher, school psychologist, special education director, and intermediate superintendent. He also co-directed the feasibility study to create the Community College known today as Montcalm Community College, where he also served as one of the first instructors. Seiter was directly involved in obtaining and getting both the Gaffield School and Caboose moved to Heritage Village. As a shaker and mover of education in the greater Montcalm area, he believes that "Heritage Village is one of, if not the finest addition to the historical value of Montcalm County" (Seiter).

Ilene Thomsen became involved with the Village when the Gaffield School was moved at the beginning, 25 years ago. She states, "It came from the Amble area where I grew up. That sparked an interest, and so I decided to become a life member" (Thomsen). Although it was the school that sparked her interest, she spent most of her time working with and in the Shoen Log House. "The cabin seemed to be a natural. I grew up in the time of many of the contents, some of which I donated!" In addition to those donations, Ilene also gave of her time getting the yard sales started, working the bake sales, and assisting wherever in the Village she was needed. She shares:

> Heritage Village gave me the friendship of many I may not have known otherwise. I believe it is a place where the youth of today can get a glimpse of yesterday and can experience a walk in their grandparent's shoes! And, it's a great place for family reunions. I also like how the bricks in front of the Village Church serve as memorials. (Thomsen)

Ilene worked for 21 years at Hitachi in Edmore, and was a Girl Scout Leader for 13 years. All three of her children attended Montcalm Community College. Today, she enjoys woodcarving and gardening.

Marge Stone-Waldron joined the Heritage Village Association in 1998 at the request of her childhood friend, Jean Brundage, who now serves as the Village Chairperson. "Jean asked me to 'join in the fun,'" she muses (Waldron). Marge assists Jean with the tours of the Sidney General Store, and is in charge of Belle's Hat Shop. She also has served as chair of the rummage sale (two years) and chair of crafts (ten years), and sends the thank you letters to Village contributors. She writes, "I have so many fond memories of working with Harriet [Olson], Phil [Frisbie], Edna [Hansen], and so many others who were great to work with. I think it is important to preserve the heritage of our area, and I have such joy in giving tours to school children" (Waldron). Marge is a retired financial planner who was born and raised in Crystal, moved away from the area for 48 years, and returned happily "to find the same great community."

Evelyn Warner first became involved with the Village when Gaffield School arrived. She proudly tells everyone that she was one of a family of seven children, and all of them attended Gaffield School for all eight grades! Her family has actually been a part of Winfield Township for over 120 years. She states, "I was a 16-year old 4-H Club Leader in 1941 when I graduated from Lakeview High School, and earned the 'I Dare You' Award. Now, I'm an 86 year-old retired factory worker who enjoys antiques and gardening, and volunteering for the Village. People who haven't visited Heritage Village don't know what they're missing" (Warner).

Dale White joined the committee 10 years ago after retiring from General Motors. He was "looking for things to do," and saw significant value in the development of Heritage Village. While his primary responsibilities have focused on the Ehle Barn and Shoen Log House, he has had a hand in the building, repairing, and/or painting of all the buildings except the Gaffield School and the Gift Shop. White expresses, "The Festivals are fun, although they are a lot of work. One year we had someone who brought two milk cows for the kids to milk by hand. They were fun to watch. Some enjoyed it, but some wouldn't even touch the cows" (D. White).

Judy White also joined with her husband 10 years ago. Judy, a "jack of all trades" has volunteered her help in many of the buildings. She mostly has enjoyed the Sidney General Store and Shoen Log House. "I like to see the enthusiasm on the faces of kids and adults when they visit these two buildings" (J. White). "I enjoy helping to educate others about the days gone by, and meeting our visitors. Plus, the fellowship of working or 'playing' at the Village is special to me." Judy also works in the food booth and yard sale during Festival. Prior to her involvement with the Village, she was a cashier and greeter at the Meijer Store for over 17 years. In her retirement, she also enjoys yard-saling, antiquing, reading, doing word searches, and spending time with her husband and grandchildren.

Miriam Zimmerman read a notice about the monthly meetings of Heritage Village just shortly before she retired as a school teacher, and decided to check it out immediately following retirement in 2000. At the first meeting she attended, she learned more about the Village and history of the buildings from Jean Brundage, Phil Frisbie, and Edna Hansen. "Our three daughters had participated in the Gaffield School during the Annual Festivals back in the 1980s when the Village consisted of only the school and the log cabin.

This drew me back as more buildings were added," Miriam muses. Over the years, she has assisted as a "teacher" at Gaffield School, helped at the Shoen Log House, assisted at the food booth in the Pavilion, and now chairs the food booth. She has also worked on gardens as a Master Gardener volunteer, and assisted with the bank lunches given for Sidney State Bank employees each year. "I enjoy sharing information about the Village with others and the access we have to so much of our county's history. I also love seeing the discoveries children make and the information they take away from their time at the Village" (Zimmerman).

Zimmerman is a retired school teacher and lives on a farm south of Carson City, where she has been for 40 years. She has three children and twelve grandchildren, and enjoys gardening, reading, puzzles, antiquing, and collecting antique butter pots and cups and saucers. The home she lives in is a 105-plus year-old farmhouse, and she has a keen interest in learning more of its history. She declares, "Heritage Village is Montcalm County's 'best kept secret.' I'd like more of our county residents to learn more about it and discover it!" (Zimmerman)

Current Docents	
Kathy Beard – *Shoen Log House*	Vivian Hey – *Sidney Town Hall*
Larry Beard – *Caboose/McBride's Depot*	Lou Kitchenmaster – *The Edmore Jail*
Mary Jane Bills – *The Village Church*	Flora Phelps – *The Doctor's House*
Jean Brundage – *Sidney General Store*	Bill Raymor – *The Blacksmith Shop*
Earl Buskirk – *The Tool Shed*	Sharon Ritter – *The Gaffield School*
Ruth Hansen – *The Caboose*	Alvin and Margaret Rush – *The Rush Dairy*
Gary Hauck – *The Village Church*	Miriam Zimmerman – *The Pavilion*

Elle Kemph greets visitors to Heritage Village. Clarence and Harriet Olson enjoy tea time inside the Town Hall. Maxine Harris waits for guests inside Shoen Log House. A guest learns the history of the Log House from Jane Raymor. Bob Milne enjoys a pre-concert planning dinner at the Clifford Lake Inn with his wife Linda, mother-in-law Carolyn Leithauser, Marilyn & Jesse Fox, and Lois Hauck. Gaffield School "pupils" pose during Heritage Festival 2010. Over 100 students enjoy a student tour during the 2011 Montcalm Community College Music Festival. Volunteers construct a new Farm Equipment Shelter.

21.

CONTRIBUTORS, MEMBERS, AND VOLUNTEERS

The Heritage Village Committee, Montcalm Community College, and members of the community wish to thank every contributor, Association member, and volunteer who has given the gifts of time, energy, skill, work and resources in the development of the Village over these past 25 years. Again, the fear in creating a list of individuals and organizations is the possibility of accidentally omitting the name or names of others who by all means should be recognized. In such cases, the Committee joins the author in begging forgiveness. With this in mind appreciation is deeply expressed to each of the following:

Ash Foundation
Big L Lumber
Blanchard Thriftway
Bookwalter Motor Sales
Brooks Electric Co.
Carson City Chamber
Carson City Lumber
Chemical Bank Montcalm
Clifford Lake Inn
Firstbank-Lakeview
FMB Commercial Bank
Greenville Community Bank (Isabella Bank)

H-M-O
Independent Bank
Isabella Bank & Trust
Ladu – Brundage Agency
Long Oil & LPL
MARSP
Marston Enterprises
Millard's Furniture & Appliance
Montcalm Area ISD
Republican Party of Montcalm Co.
Sidney State Bank
Stanton Rotary Club/Jim Lantz
Stanton Women's Club

Stebbins & Simpson Funeral

Stebbins-McCullough Chapel

The Village Market Group

VFW Auxilary

VFW Sheridan

Helen Aagaard

Glen Ackley, Jr.

Clyde Adams

Laverne Adams

Margaret Adams

Natalie Adams

Mrs. Jake Allies

Mrs. Bud Alsgaard

Roy Anderson

Stewart Anderson

Larry Anstette

Ivan W. Arntz

Mike Arntz

Rosalie Ashbaugh

Susan J. Avery

Helen Bailey

Wilma Baldwin

Helen Beachler

Lois Beal

Barbara Beard

Mr. & Mrs. Lawrence Beard

Dr. & Mrs. Clifford Bedore

Denise Beebe

Maxine Bell

Norva Bennett

Tony Benson Family

Mr. & Mrs. Fred Bernat

Freida Best

Phillip Bigler

Mary Jane Bills

Marvel Bissell

Betty Blanchard

Carman Blatt

Elbert Boes

Berwin Bow

Rev. Bob Braman

Mr. & Mrs. Charles Braman

Mr. & Mrs. J. W. Brand

Gloria Noll Brendle

Ann Brody

Mr. & Mrs. Robert Brooks

Mr. & Mrs. Bill Brown

Mr. & Mrs. Harry Brown

Mr. & Mrs. Larry Brundage

Mr. & Mrs. Robert Brundage

R.J. Brune

Mr. & Mrs. Harry Bruno

Mr. & Mrs. Kenneth Brygal

Rita Brygal

Mr. & Mrs. Al Buchholz

Rene Buenterle

Dr. & Mrs. Leo Bunce

Mary Bunce

Richard Burke

Mr. & Mrs. Everett Burkey

Dr. & Mrs. Donald Burns

Kenneth Burns

Mary Burns

Earl Buskirk

Robert Buskirk

Shirley Buskirk

Mr. & Mrs. James Butler

Robert Button

Lois Caldwell

Rick Calkins

Mr. & Mrs. Larry Carbonelli

Anna Carstensen

Nancy Carter
John Chapin
Mr. & Mrs. Carl Chapin
Russell Chester
Mr. & Mrs. Bruce Christensen
Eldon Christensen
Geraldine Christensen
Mrs. Leroy Christensen
Harold Christiansen
Bryce Christoffersen
Lillian Christophersen
Mr. & Mrs. Bill Ciganik
Grace Clementz
Rachel Clementz
Kelly Clevenger
Anita Colby
Terri Coleman
Peggy Conner
Doris McConnell Cook
Mr. & Mrs. Gerald Cook
Mr. & Mrs. Kevin Cook
Theron Comden
Mr. & Mrs. Ken Cory
Elaine Crawford
Quinten Cusack
Mr. & Mrs. Claude Dale
Mr. & Mrs. Alan Davis
Bea Dawes
Vera DeGood
Thelma Dell
Bruce Dennis
Bernie DeSpelder
Mr. & Mrs. Don Dingman
Michele Dykstra
Dorothy Eggleston
Margaret Eggleston

Ed Ehle Jr.
Edward Ehle
Mr. & Mr. Fred Ehle
Joyce Ehle
Mr. & Mrs. William Ellsworth
Mr. & Mrs. Burl Emmons
Larry Engle
Maynard Failing
Bonita Flint
Phyllis Foote
Mr. & Mrs. Jesse Fox
Mr. & Mrs. Phil Frisbie
Nancy Gale
Brian Gardner
Florence Gavitt
Janet Gerlach
Mr. & Mrs. Ivan Gharring
Dave Gillette
Mike Gommesen Family
Gordon Green
Dorothy Guericki
Mrs. Gutka
Mr. & Mrs. Carl Hacker
Clayton Hadley
Elaine Hadley
Mr. & Mrs. Charles Halterman
Donald Hansen
Earl Hansen
Edna Hansen
Kathryn Hansen
Lillian Hansen
Margarette Hansen
Nicki Hansen
Ruth Hansen
Mr. & Mrs. Allen Hardy
Irene Hardy

Judy Hardy

Maxine Harris

Greg Harrison

Ann Hart

Mr. & Mrs. Clare Hart

Mr. & Mrs. Thayer Hart

Dr. & Mrs. Gary Hauck

Mr. & Mrs. Greg Hauck

George Hendrick

Donald Hendrickson

Vivian Hey

Margaret Hill

Maureen Hockstra

Mr. & Mrs. Holger Holm

Norma Horn

Kathrene Hosner

Betty Houle

Joyce Howell

Mr. & Mrs. Leon Howell

Mr. & Mrs. Dale Hubbs

Gladys Ingalls

Lucille Jensen

M. Jensen

Mr. & Mrs. Chester Jensen

Mr. & Mrs. Elton Jensen

Barbara Johnson

Eloise Johnson

Mr. & Mrs. Chester Johnson

Elaine Johnson

Janet Johnson

Mr. & Mrs. Paul Johnson

Robert S. Johnson

Tina Jones

Mr. & Mrs. Stan Jorgensen

William Jorgensen

Mike Karasinski

Rita Kellogg

Mr. & Mrs. Randy Kempf

Shannon Kilduff

Colleen Kiley

Natalie Kilfoil

Keith King

Ralph Kinsey

Ron Kinsey

Lou Kitchenmaster

Virginia Knepper

Mr. & Mrs. Alan Kohn

Linda Kohn

Mr. & Mrs. Ted Kortes

Dorothy Krampe

Deborah Kreitner

Mr. & Mrs. Charles Krug

Tim Krug

Bernie Kulas

Marge Kutzke

Alice Lance

Bethel Larsen

JoAnne Larson

Mary Ann Last

Carol Lau

Mr. & Mrs. Tom Learmont

Gail Lehman

Eleanor Lentz

Donald Linebaugh

Margaret Long

Rosemary Long

Crystal Lund

Mr. & Mrs. Donald Lund

Charles Lyons

Valgene Mack

Mr. & Mrs. Paul Mahan

Mr .& Mrs. Richard Main

Mr. & Mrs. Gerald Malling

Dorothy Marks

Bob Marston

Judy McAlvey

Mr. & Mrs. Keith McInnis

Lucille McLachlan

Mr. & Mrs. Tom McLachlen

Mr. & Mrs. Robert McNutt

Janice Meek

Mr. & Mrs. Fred Meijer

Harry Middleton

Charles Miel

Mr. & Mrs. Homer Miel

Mr. & Mrs. Charles Miller

Rand Miller

Donna Moore

Lucille Moore

Les Morford

Lee Myers

Jack Nelson

Nancy N'Gele

Barbara Nielsen

Calvin Nielsen

Mary Lou Nielsen

Sara Nutt

Mr. & Mrs. Ed O'Brien

Sue O'Brien

Mark Olsen

Mr. and Mrs. Clarence Olson

Marcela Ort

Dr. & Mrs. Robert Painter

Barbara Parker

Fayga Parker

Emma Patmore

Irene Patrick

Larry Pearson

Doris Pellow

Esther Petersen

Evella Petersen

Jody Petersen

Judy Petersen

Ruth Ann Petersen

Mr. & Mrs. Max Phelps

JoAnn Porter

Janet Potte

David Pritchard

Evelyn Pritchard

Ruth Proctor

Gary Randall

Mr. & Mrs. George Ranney

Bob Rasmussen

Richard Ravell

Rev. & Mrs. William Raymor

Mr. & Mrs. Hugh Reed

Mr. & Mrs. Ken Reed

Velma Reed

Frank Reeder

Mr. & Mrs. Rex Rice

Virginia Reynolds

Geraldine Rice

Mrs. Gerry Rice

Mr. & Mrs. Arthur Ritter

Mr. & Mrs. Gerald Ritter

Patricia Rockafellow

Mr. & Mrs. Ernest Rogers

Winnefred Roody

Margaret Roper

Mable Rose

Virginia Rose

Mr. &. Mrs. Vernon Wayne Ross

Isabel Rossman

Lida Rossman

Mrs. William Rowe

Margaret Royer

Mr. & Mrs. Alvin Rush

Mary Russell

Eugene Rydahl

Joyce Sage

Georgia Schad

Mr. & Mrs. Rusty Schlentz

Bonnie Schlosser

Marilyn Sieb

Dr. & Mrs. William Seiter

Virginia Sharp

Barney Shoen

Steve Shoen

Elizabeth Smith

Hazel Smith

Lillian Smith

Mr. & Mrs. Mike Smith

Phyllis E. Smith

Ruth Smith

Virginia Snyder

Mr. & Mrs. Ron Springsteen

Mr. & Mrs. Harold Springsteen

Marjory Staines

Donald Stearns

Betty Steere

James Steere

Kristie Steere

Roy Story

Irene Stowell

Hilla Strom

Evelyn Sturdavent

Diane Sutherland

Florence Taylor

Robert Taylor

Peg Terry

Mr. & Mrs. Martin Thompsen

Josie Thompson

Margarite Thompson

Ilene Thomsen

Rose Ellen Thomsen

Dorothy Trexler

Linda Troop

Naomi & Carolyn Tubbs

Betty Turner

Frank Tuttle

Mr. & Mrs. Richard Vanderlip

Mr. & Mrs. Jim Veresh

Roy Vertergaard

Mr. & Mrs. Tony Vovides

Al Waldorf

Dick Waldorf

Marge Stone-Waldron

Mr. & Mrs. Roger Waldron

Mr. & Mrs. Dean Walldorf

Robin Walter

Evelyn Warner

Mr. & Mrs. Dale White

Willidean Whitmore

Doris Whitten

James Wilcox

Roger Wilcox

Loraine Williamson

Mr. & Mrs. Howard Wilson

Lori Wilson

Phoebe Wilson

Sarah Wojtowicz

Ryan Wolf

Sandy Woodcock

Mr. & Mrs. Paul Worden

Mr. & Mrs. Melbourne Worfel

Olga Wright

Mr. & Mrs. Larry Yaw
Mary Zarback
Mr. & Mrs. Bob Zimmerman
Mr. & Mrs. Ike Zimmerman
Jean Zimmerman

Epilogue –
Montcalm Community College Today

Just as Heritage Village has developed significantly over the course of these 25 years, so has the parent organization of Montcalm Community College. Today, MCC draws nearly 2,500 credit and non-credit students, and participates in the Michigan Community College Virtual Learning Collaborative. It awards five degrees with more than 20 occupational majors, 18 certificate programs, and more than 20 job training certificates. MCC's campus has grown to include nine buildings in addition to Heritage Village. Its faculty in the 2010-2011 academic year included 28 full-time and 107 part-time (adjunct) instructors, and the staff had 72 full-time and 108 part-time members.

Recently, Dr. Donald Burns retired after 25 successful years as president, and MCC's fifth president, Robert Ferrentino J.D., led the institution through the groundwork for a new three-year strategic plan, building on that foundation. In the MCC publication, *Strategic Plan for 2010-2013*, Ferrentino shares the revised Vision, Mission, and Values Statements that were facilitated as a collaborative work of trustees, staff, faculty, students, and community members:

Vision

Montcalm Community College is west-central Michigan's preeminent provider of and preferred choice for education, training, and lifelong learning opportunities.

Mission

MCC is a leader in creating a learning community, contributing to shared economic, cultural, and social prosperity for our citizens.

Values

Montcalm Community College subscribes to the following institutional values:

- We provide a caring environment for our students, staff, and community.
- We expect competence and the pursuit of excellence from our students and staff.
- We work in concert with our stakeholder communities to advance the philosophy of lifelong learning.
- We are committed to providing open access and fostering success for all of our learners. (Ferrentino, *Strategic Plan* 2-3)

President Ferrentino also appreciates the role that Heritage Village plays in the overall mission of the college and in keeping with the institution's values. He reflects:

When I first arrived on MCC's campus in the summer of 2009, I was impressed by many features of the campus. The beautiful rural setting is highlighted by state-of the-art facilities, plenty of green space, a peaceful nature trail, and numerous other amenities that make the campus feel like home.

During my first two weeks on campus, I was the beneficiary of not one, but two, guided tours of the Heritage Village. I quickly began to see the special value of the Village, not only in the historical buildings, but also in the stories behind the buildings – in the people who made the history of Montcalm County, and in the preservation of those peoples' stories.

Heritage Village takes us all back to simpler time in our history. Wandering through the village, one can imagine what it must have been like to work behind the counter of the general store selling penny candy or shoeing your neighbors' horses in the blacksmith shop. I think about the old "shave and a haircut, two bits" line and wonder if waiting your turn in that barber shop held any resemblance to today's hustle and bustle world.

This exposure to the history of Montcalm County, right on our campus, was more than a small surprise to me. I think about the people who had the vision to begin this labor of love so many years ago and I know we are fortunate that they had the courage to carry the vision to reality. Heritage Village stands as a testament to our forefathers, enabling today's citizens to develop a new appreciation for the struggles and perseverance of our ancestors.

I think of Heritage Village as a valued asset for the people of Montcalm County. I am proud to show visitors the Village and brag that MCC is the only community college in the state to have worked so diligently to preserve the past in such a way so that we all may learn from it and improve upon it.

Today, we at MCC consistently seek to set the tone for our future by improving upon our past. We have implemented a new strategic plan that holds the promise of improving student success rates, reaching out in more proactive ways to our community, and building upon our already existing base of quality instruction and community programming. Our campus commitment to student success has been reenergized by our participation in the national *Achieving the Dream* initiative.

Budgetary struggles are a fact of life for most public institutions in today's world of declining financial support at both the state and local levels. MCC is no exception. The loss of good-paying manufacturing jobs, precipitated by the closing of key industrial sites in our region, has hit our community hard over the past decade. The state of Michigan has struggled mightily to stem the growing tide of unemployment and outward migration of talented workers. It is an exciting, albeit challenging time to work in higher education.

The good news is that we are well-positioned for the future. We have a dedicated staff of talented professionals with the requisite skills to help us achieve the goals we've established for ourselves. Construction projects are in the works that will transform our M-TEC in Greenville and dramatically improve the energy efficient operation of the college's main campus in Sidney. Curriculum developments have brought new programs of study for our students which will result in new career opportunities for them.

It is indeed an exciting time to work in the world of education. We at Montcalm Community College embrace these times as we simultaneously look ahead and plan the College's future contributions to our region's collective prosperity. Please join us in the effort; feel free to drop by the campus anytime. The doors are open and we are ready to meet and surpass the community's expectations. (Ferrentino e-mail)

It is evident that the new leadership of MCC strongly desires to maintain the relationship between Heritage Village and Montcalm Community College, and foster the ongoing development of both. Today, MCC's summer camps include tours and activities at Heritage Village; the Annual MCC Music Festival brings well over a hundred students from throughout the county to the Village for tours; and college courses have been launched in Local History and Heritage that will explore the history and story of Heritage Village. While seeking to preserve the autonomy of the Heritage Village Association, Montcalm Community College looks forward to new and creative ways of enjoying this educational partnership, and to many anniversaries ahead with mutual celebration.

Works Cited

Beard, Kathleen. Letter to the author. 8 Feb. 2011. Handwritten.

Beard, Larry. Letter to the author. 8 Mar. 2011. Handwritten.

Bedore, Ruth. Letter to the author. 18 Apr. 2011. Handwritten.

Benson, Tony. Telephone interview. 30 Mar. 2011.

Brigham, Steve. Telephone interview. 13 Apr. 2011.

Brundage, Jean. Letter to the author. 19 Mar. 2011. Handwritten.

Brundage, Jean. Personal communication. 22 Apr. 2011.

Brundage, Jean. Personal interview. 12 Nov. 2010.

Brundage, Jean. Telephone interview. 13 Apr. 2011.

Burns, Donald C. Personal interview. 9 Feb. 2011.

Buskirk, Robert. Letter to the author. 1 Mar. 2011. Typescript.

Buskirk, Robert. Telephone interview. 12 Apr. 2011.

Christensen, Geraldine. Letter to the author. 21 Feb. 2011. Handwritten.

Christensen, Linda. "Area Couple Celebrate 75 Years of Marital Bliss." *The Daily News* [Greenville, MI] 16 Jan. 1997. Sec. 1:6+. Print.

Christophersen, Lillian. Letter to the author. 5 Mar. 2011. Handwritten.

Ferrentino, Bob. "Heritage Village." Message to the author. 29 Apr. 2011. E-mail.

Ferrentino, Bob. *Strategic Plan for 2010-2012*. Sidney, MI: Montcalm Community College, 2010. Print.

Fox, Jesse. Letter to the author. 16 Feb. 2011. Handwritten.

Fox, Jesse. Telephone interview. 11 Apr. 2011.

Fox, Marilyn. Letter to the author. 16 Feb. 2011. Handwritten.

Germain, David L. Letter to Jean Brundage. 15 Jan. 2006. Typescript.

Germain, George. Personal communication. 15 Feb. 2011.

Harris, Maxine. Letter to the author. 1 Mar. 2011. Handwritten.

Hedrick, Jody. Telephone interview. 29 Apr. 2011.

Heritage Village. *Constitution of the Heritage Village Committee, Inc.* Sidney: MI: Montcalm Community College, n.d. Print.

Heritage Village. *School Days*. Sidney, MI: Montcalm Community College, 1987. Print.

Hey, Vivien. Letter to the author. 14 Mar. 2011. Handwritten.

Hey, Vivian. Telephone interview. 30 Mar. 2011.

Lantz, James. Personal interview. 21 Jan. 2011.

Lau, Eric. Telephone interview. 30 Mar. 2011.

Learmont, Tom. Personal interview. 15 Oct. 2010.

Learmont, Tom. Letter to the author. 22 Feb. 2011. Typescript.

Mack, Kathleen. Letter to the author. 1 Mar. 2011. Handwritten.

Mahan, Mildred. Letter to the author. 13 Feb. 2011. Handwritten.

Marston, Bob. Letter to the author. 23 Feb. 2011. Handwritten.

Meyers, Jeffrey. "Heritage Gets Extra Attention at Festival." *The Daily News* [Greenville, MI] 3 Aug. 1991. Sec. 1:1+. Print.

Miller, Rand. Telephone interview. 30 Mar. 2011.

Milne, Bob. "Heritage Village Book." Message to the author. 2 Mar. 2011. E-mail.

Milne, Bob. *The Journeyman Piano Player*. Lapeer, MI: Woodland Press, 1992. Print.

Montcalm Community College – Creating Brighter Futures – Catalog 2009-2011. Sidney, MI:

Montcalm Community College, 2009. Print.

Montcalm Heritage Village – Where History is More than a Picture. Sidney, MI: Montcalm Heritage Village, n.d. Print.

Olson, Harriett, ed. *The Story of the North Sidney Area 1884-1994*. Sidney, MI: North Sidney Church and Cemetery Historical Association, 1984. Print.

Paris, Jim. "Re: Heritage Village Questionnaire." Message to the author. 22 Feb. 2011. E-mail.

Phelps, Flora. "Heritage Village." Message to the author. 21 Mar. 2011. E-mail.

Phelps, Max. "Heritage Village." Message to the author, 21Mar. 2011. E-mail.

Richland Township Scrapbook, Retained in Heritage Village Town Hall, n.d.

Ritter, Sharon. Letter to the author. 17 Feb. 2011. Handwritten.

Rush, Alvin. "Heritage Village." Message to the author, 21 Mar. 2011. E-mail.

Rush, Margaret. "Heritage Village." Message to the author, 21 Mar. 2011. E-mail.

Rydahl, Eugene. Letter to the author. 2 Mar. 2011. Handwritten.

Seiter, William. Letter to the author. 22 Feb. 2011. Typescript.

Shoen, Barney. Letter to the author. 19 Feb. 2011. Handwritten.

Sidney Township Scrapbook, 2 vols. Retained in Heritage Village Town Hall, n.d.

Smith, Terry, sec. Heritage Village Committee official minutes, 1987-1992.

Smith, Terry. Personal communication. 19 Feb. 2011.

Thomsen, Ilene. Letter to the author. 24 Feb. 2011. Handwritten.

Village Church Guestbook, Retained in the Heritage Village Church foyer, n.d. Handwritten.

Waldron, Marge Stone-. Letter to the author. 17 Mar. 2011. Handwritten.

Warner, Evelyn. Letter to the author. 19 Mar. 2011. Handwritten.

Wendell, C. H. *Encyclopedia of American Farm Implements and Antiques.* 2nd ed. Lola, WI: Krause Pub., 2004. Print.

White, Dale. Letter to the author. 15 Feb. 2011. Handwritten.

White, Judy. Letter to the author. 16 Feb. 2011. Handwritten.

Wood, Ronald M. "Historic White Pine Village," Mason County Historical Society, 2011. Web. 7 Mar. 2011. www.historicwhitepinevillage.org/

Zimmerman, Miriam. Letter to the author. 9 Mar. 2011. Handwritten.

Zimmerman, Miriam. Telephone interview. 30 Mar. 2011.

About the Author

Dr. Gary L. Hauck is a member of the Heritage Village Committee and serves as Dean of Instruction and Faculty at Montcalm Community College in Sidney, Michigan, where he also teaches humanities, religion, and history. He holds a PhD from Michigan State University and received MSU's Richard L. Featherstone Award and Donald O. Tatroe Award for Scholarship. Most recently, he is the recipient of the 2011 Montcalm Community College Leadership Award.

Hauck is a member of the Montcalm Area Art Association, Mid-Michigan Arts Council, Flat River Historical Society, and the Advisory Board of the World Affairs Council of Western Michigan. He is the co-chair of One Book One County – Montcalm, and has served on the Board of the Montcalm Area Reading Council. Currently, Hauck is endeavoring to establish the Montcalm Area Council for the Humanities.

As a lover of the humanities, Gary has traveled to all 50 states and 44 countries, leading student groups to many of these. He has taught college courses in China, Ecuador, and Russia, and has participated in archeological digs in the Middle East. Hauck is the author of 14 books including, *Organizational Education in Higher Education,* and *Exploring Humanities Around the World.*

Married for 39 years to Lois Thornton (author of *The Caregiver,* and co-author with Gary of *Spiritual Formation*), the Haucks live in West Michigan and have four children: Heidi, Greg (& Rachel), Andrew (& Becky), and Jared; and one grandchild, Jacob Andrew.